Pen Duick

Also by Eric Tabarly

LONELY VICTORY

Eric Tabarly

Pen Duick

Translated by Len Ortzen

Adlard Coles Limited   London

Granada Publishing Limited
First published in Great Britain 1971 by Adlard Coles Limited
3 Upper James Street London W1R 4BP

De Pen Duick en Pen Duick first published in France 1970
by Editions Arthaud, Paris

Copyright © B Arthaud 1970
This translation copyright © Adlard Coles Limited 1971

ISBN 0 229 98647 1
Printed in Great Britain by
C. Tinling & Co. Ltd, London and Prescot

Contents

Preface

Of Eric Tabarly as a seaman there is no need to write. His reputation is international. He speaks for himself in these pages with a total lack of egotism, while telling an adventurous story with delightful detachment.

But one side of his achievement is less widely appreciated; naturally, because it demands specialised knowledge. He is, among practical seamen of outstanding practical achievement, the most radical and daring experimentalist in the types of sailing craft he uses for his exploits. Quite casually in the pages below he describes the conceptions and the performances of Pen Duick III, IV and V, which followed the comparatively conventional, but much experimented on, Pen Duick II.

I remember seeing for the first time Pen Duick III from the starting platform of the Royal Ocean Racing Club's Morgan Cup race in 1967. She caused surprise among some of us – a big, rather ugly aluminium yacht carrying a remarkable version of the schooner rig hardly recognised by the rules, and crewed by a multitude. And this, it seemed possible then, was to be his boat in the next year's Singlehanded Transatlantic Race. He had, of course, won the race with Pen Duick II in 1964.

Then one evening later in the Royal Ocean Racing Club someone produced, with the air of one springing a surprise, a photograph of Pen Duick IV's model. This amazing 65 foot trimaran was the craft Tabarly chose for the Transatlantic Race in preference to Pen Duick III, perhaps unfortunately. Then came Pen Duick V, a reversion to the single hull type, but conventional in no other respect, with movable water ballast and a planing capability that brought success in the Transpacific Race.

Now we await for the surprise of Pen Duick VI.

Douglas Phillips-Birt

Part One

The Demon of Racing

1

Pen Duick II
gets her
second wind

After winning the singlehanded Transatlantic race in 1964 I made up my mind to go on racing. The boat with which I had won, Pen Duick II, had not been conceived for handicap races and I was used to racing with a crew. However, I had proof of several of the boat's qualities, in particular her capacity for beating to windward in a stiff breeze and especially in rough weather. Although I had not been able to compare her with other boats, it seemed to me that the worse the weather the better she sailed when close hauled or with a following wind. On the other hand she seemed to perform rather poorly in light airs.

I was thinking of sailing back to France from Newport after the race, as I had not the money to ship Pen Duick II home and buy an air or even steamer ticket for myself. But then the French shipping line, the Compagnie Générale Transatlantique, very kindly offered to transport my boat on board the cargo vessel Carbé and to give me equally free passage on the liner France. I gratefully jumped at the offer, for I should thus be back in France in time to take part in the last two important races of the season – the Yarmouth to Santander and the Santander to La Trinité. This mattered greatly to me, for these ocean races would enable me to compare Pen Duick II with other boats, which was much more interesting for future plans than just crossing the Atlantic on my own. I should thus be able to verify whether my opinion of Pen Duick II was correct. I knew that the boat's failings when the wind was slight (due in part to being under-canvassed for singlehanded sailing) meant that I could not hope to win unless rough weather was encountered.

Pen Duick II was unloaded at Le Havre and I at once asked for an official measurer of the Royal Ocean racing Club, which was the organizer of the two races, to come and rate her handicap. This is done by taking certain measurements which are multiplied or divided according to a single formula for each and every competitor. In this way, widely different craft can be raced together – though not with an even chance of success for every competitor, contrary to the good

1 Pen Duick II under jib and mizzen during the 1964 Transatlantic race

intentions of the inventors of the formula. Exact evaluation of the factors which cause a boat to sail fast and those which slow her down is too difficult for estimating their correct worth in the formula. Therefore the handicap ruling is not perfect, and for a boat to compete with the maximum chance she needs to be designed with the ruling in mind. This is what boat designers have been doing for years. So there is a problem of design at the very beginning, to build a boat which can be sailed as fast as possible for her handicap rating. A compromise has to be found – an interesting mental exercise and quite amusing.

For instance, to what extent should one increase a measurement which the handicap formula penalizes but which makes the boat speedier? Would the penalty be greater than the gain in speed? Conversely, by extending another characteristic would the gain on handicap sufficiently compensate for the loss in speed?

The average wind conditions likely to be met during these races have also to be taken into account, for then one can estimate how many square feet of canvas to give the boat. As this sail area is the driving force, obviously the larger it is the more the boat will be penalized. So if there is too much and one had to take in sail too often, because of hardening winds, one would have been excessively handicapped for a sail area put to use only half the time; and one's chances would depend on the winds being light. Conversely, if there is not enough canvas,

more advantage would be lost in light winds than is gained by the favourable handicap; and one's chances would depend on the winds being strong.

It can thus be seen that designing an ocean racer is a complicated and very interesting problem calling for considerable sailing experience and knowledge. Much thought and ingenuity is applied to designing for maximum performance within the rules.

The start of the Yarmouth to Santander race was on August 8, so there was no time to lose if we were going to take part in it. Pen Duick II set sail for England without having visited her home port – where everyone was eager to see her, as I realised on returning there from Santander.

In the early stages of the race Pen Duick II, beating into a Force 6 wind, was soon ahead of all the other boats of her class (II). They had all taken in a reef or two but we had not and were going well. The big class I boat, Outlaw, well known for her qualities in sailing close to the wind, was only slowly drawing away from us. If only it stayed like that! But it didn't stay like that for long. Weather conditions changed on the

2 Pen Duick II running before the wind. Transatlantic 1964

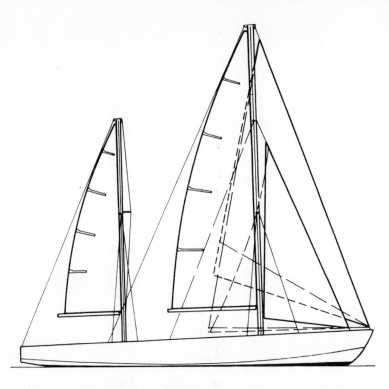

3 Pen Duick II sail
plan for the Transatlantic
race
Mainsail: 230 sq ft
Mizzen: 107 sq ft
Genoa: 354 sq ft
No 1 Yankee: 320 sq ft
No 2 Yankee: 253 sq ft
Genoa jib: 177 sq ft
Storm jib: 120 sq ft

first night, it fell calm and, as expected, we were overtaken and left astern by many of the competitors. We had only light or moderate winds all the way to Santander and finished about halfway down class II.

For the return, Santander to La Trinité, we had a good wind abeam right from the start and weren't doing too badly. Then it began to blow a Force 7 gale and we fairly scudded along. We took the lead, with Outlaw second. But alas, I made an error in navigation which resulted in our arriving at La Trinité among the tail-enders.

However, these two races had at least proved to me that the boat performed very well at all points of sailing in strong winds, but very poorly when the wind was light.

The solution was to increase the sail area (3). Her handicap would be greater, but this would be compensated for in strong winds, and the need of faster sailing in light winds was all-important. As I was thinking of building a new boat which would be longer than Pen Duick II, and to have her schooner rigged in order to divide up the sail area better for singlehanded sailing, I decided to try out this rig on Pen Duick II. I would then see how she performed in ocean races. This conversion had the advantage of not being too costly, for the mainmast

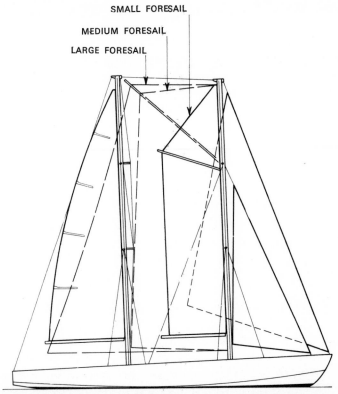

SMALL FORESAIL

MEDIUM FORESAIL

LARGE FORESAIL

4 Pen Duick II
schooner rigged
Mainsail: 230 sq ft
Small foresail: 215 sq ft
Medium foresail: 440 sq ft
Large foresail: 676 sq ft
Headsails as before

5 Pen Duick II schooner
rigged, close hauled and
carrying the smallest
foresail. The two larger
foresails were only used
when the wind was
abeam or on the quarter

would remain where it was and as it was and become the foremast. I should only have to replace the mizzen with a taller mast stepped farther forward, which would become the mainmast. Schooner rig had been rather given up for ocean racing, as it was thought this rig was not so efficient as others. But I believed that to be true only for heavy craft.

Pen Duick II was converted during the winter (4,5) and I received an offer for her from the State School of Sailing at Beg-Rohy. I accepted, as I was going to need money to build Pen Duick III. But in the meantime I continued to sail Pen Duick II. She was put afloat again in the spring of 1965, to take part in some minor, early season races at La Rochelle and one or two Breton yachting centres.

The conversion had not been thought much of by my sailing friends, but they soon changed their opinion when we won all these races. We were lucky, it is true, in having favourable weather conditions for the boat, whereas results in more important races later in the season were far from brilliant, with the exception of a very good placing in the Cowes to Dinard race on July 9. Pen Duick II sailed much better, but still had her weak points, especially when running before a light wind. This was due to the lack of area in the triangle of headsails – I had not altered these sails, in order to make the conversion as cheaply as possible and the spinnaker was too small. However, these races had shown at any rate that the schooner rig was quite valid; but the present ratio was not ideal – the sail area between the masts would have to be reduced in favour of the headsails. So I was beginning to have a good idea, thanks to these experiences, of the most suitable rig for Pen Duick III.

Meanwhile, Pen Duick II was converted for a second time. I realised that she was still not at her maximum efficiency. Moreover, I intended to race her in American waters the following season, and the handicap rulings over there are very different from the English. So modifications were necessary for these reasons, and were carried out on the hull as well as the rigging. Pen Duick II had a long raking stern which increased her handicap under both American and English methods of measurements. So I had it cut back and made into a sloping transom, thus reducing the weight a little and gaining half a foot on her handicap, which was quite valuable. This modification proved to have no effect on her speed and, moreover, reduced her tendency to gripe when heeling sharply. Unfortunately the effect was not so good from an aesthetic point of view.

The schooner rig was changed for a ketch rig (6,7), but quite different from her original rig. The aim was to increase the sail area forward. The foremast would remain where it was; I intended just to

MULE

GENOA (CCA)
GHOSTER
YANKEE No 1
YANKEE No 2

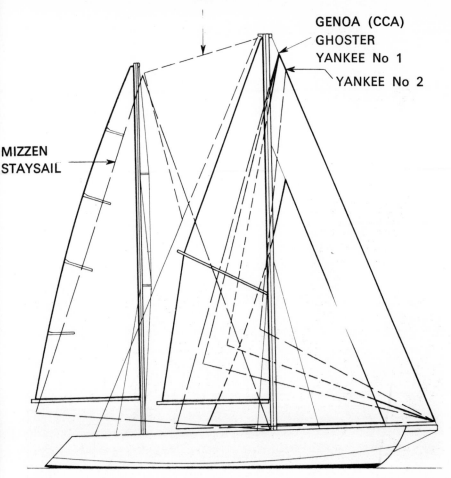

MIZZEN
STAYSAIL

increase the height. I decided also to have a foresail boom, which allowed the sail area to be increased considerably; the spinnakers, too, were increased from 750 to 1200 square feet. The mainmast was replaced, though neither the position nor the height was changed. The complete modification of the shrouds meant that this new mizzen became independent of the foremast instead of supporting it, and therefore I had a much slimmer one than before, which was better for the weight problem and offered less wind resistance.

Previously, with the schooner rig, I had two foresails each with a wishbone spar. The large one had taken all the space between the two masts and even overlapped the mainsail when on a reach or when close hauled in a slight breeze. The small foresail was very narrow for sailing into the wind. For the former, the wishbone spar now allowed a large spread of canvas to be set in a following wind, and for the latter it

6 Pen Duick II
bermudan rigged
Wishbone
mainsail: 255 sq ft
Mizzen: 230 sq ft
Genoa foresail: 543 sq ft
Ghoster: 410 sq ft
No 1 Yankee: 365 sq ft
No 2 Yankee: 270 sq ft
Genoa jib: 244 sq ft
Mule: 102 sq ft
Staysail: 457 sq ft

7 Pen Duick II ketch
rigged for the third time

allowed an appropriate amount of canvas, yet plenty of space was left
between the leech and the mainsail. This is an important point when
beating, because otherwise the foresail would take the wind out of the
sail aft. This was why, when changing to a ketch rig, I kept the
wishbone spar in order to have a fairly large mainsail which would not
hinder the mizzen.

There was another reason too. Under the American measurement,
there had to be a certain minimum area of mainsail in relation to the
height of the mast, otherwise one's handicap suffered. So it was the
only way of having that minimum area while retaining the space
between the two sails that I was set on having.

The first race at La Trinité (8) in the early spring of 1966 showed that
Pen Duick II sailed very well indeed with this new rig, and that the
speed and handicap compromise had never been so favourable to her

– at least, where the English measurement was concerned. It remained to be seen about the American.

The boat was going to take part in American races in the summer, so I decided to sail her across singlehanded. It would be useful training for the next Transatlantic race (1968).

In order to keep the new suit of sails for racing, I used the old ones which had served with the original ketch rig. The masts were now too tall for them, and the standing rigging was more ample too, so that the old sails looked rather ridiculous.

I was trying out a new kind of self-steering gear invented by Monsieur Gianoli, who had provided me with the one I used in the 1964 Transatlantic race. As the boat now had a forward-sloping transom, the device had to be mounted on a support.

I sailed from La Trinité in March. The wind was blowing from the west and during the night it hardened considerably. I soon found that the boat was leaking in an alarming manner, even for this rough weather. The reason, I discovered, was that the forward ventilator was letting in water as well as air. In the course of changing the rig and increasing the sail area forward, I must have brought the jib stay more forward, and its anchor plate was blocking the ventilator's water vent. There was nothing to be done but to pierce another opening and to put back for a proper repair job.

I remained at La Trinité for a few days until the very bad weather had given over, then I set sail again with a strong nor'wester blowing. If it held, so much the better, for I should have it abeam. The northern route across the Atlantic was not favourable at this early season because of the prevalence of westerlies, so I had chosen the Azores route. Unfortunately the nor'wester did not hold for long. In fact I hardly had Belle Ile astern than I was close hauled, and so I stayed all the way to Horta, in the Azores, where I put in nine days after leaving La Trinité. What with the Force 6 south-westerly winds and the cold of the first few days, it had not been a comfortable crossing.

However, I had a pleasant time at Horta. The Portuguese were very friendly; some of the islanders have become quite accustomed to welcoming yachtsmen, as many put in there. In fact the owner of the Sports Café, Peter, is a good Samaritan to all of us.

While there, I checked some of the gear and fittings. The self-steering gear, which was an experimental model, had worked very well apart from some play in the supports to the wind vane. I fixed this by making some shock absorbers with rings cut from a rubber inner tube and packed tightly over a bolt. I had no more trouble for the rest of the crossing.

After leaving Horta it was sunny and very warm nearly all the time. Hurrah for the lower latitudes! The crossing was uneventful until just before sighting land, when I ran into thick fog, a not uncommon occurrence off the east coast of the United States. The alarming thing was that the area is always busy with shipping into and out of New York. I stayed awake all night, listening for foghorns; but most of them sounded at a fair distance and I did not feel anxious. There was very little wind and I was moving at about two knots in a long swell. Soon after daybreak, when I had heard nothing for some time and was feeling easy in my mind, I was suddenly startled by a loud siren quite close. Where was she? I didn't know what to do. When you hear a signal in the distance which gradually draws nearer, you can at least get a rough idea of the vessel's course; but in this instance I was at a loss. In any case, moving at only two knots, there was little I could do. On the off chance, as the foghorn was within reach, I sounded the regulation signal of a sailing vessel on the starboard tack. A few seconds later I caught the sound of a ship's engines. The danger was not far off. I continued sounding the foghorn, but purely for form's sake, there being very little chance of anyone hearing it.

In a few moments I saw the stem of a ship pierce the fog on my port bow. She was less than a hundred yards away and coming straight at me, looking huge. I told myself the situation was hopeless, but no sooner had the thought flashed through my mind than I realised the ship was stopped. Ouf! She gradually emerged from the fog as I approached, and I saw that she was not so huge after all, just a big trawler. I slowly passed her bows and then she got under way again. I heard no fog signals and supposed she must have radar. They must have seen me on their screen at the last minute, stopped engines or probably gone astern even, then sounded the siren which had startled me out of my complacency.

It may well have been my metal masts which had saved me from being run down. I remember that when serving on a minesweeper in the Channel, yachts with metal masts gave a better signal on our radar screen than those with just a radar reflector, although in each case the signals were very weak. A yacht with wooden masts and without a reflector gave no signal at all. But a yacht with a metal hull gave a very good signal – an important safety measure.

The fog persisted all that day, and I entered Long Island Sound blindly, steering by radio direction finder and fog signals from light-ships and beacons. The fog lifted during the night and I saw some lights here and there, but before long a heavy storm blacked everything out again. It was the worst thunderstorm I've ever experienced – in the United States even storms are the biggest in the world. For five hours the rain pelted down and the flashes of lightning were so terrific that they lit up everything as though it were day. When my eyes happened to catch a flash I was dazzled for several seconds. And all the time the thunder rumbled and crashed, the wind kept shifting and blew from all points of the compass, strong one minute and dropping to a calm the next. It was enough to send anyone crazy. I was constantly changing tack or gybing to try and keep heading in the right direction, but without much success, and I should think that at best I managed to stay at the same spot during the whole of the storm. I may even have lost ground. And yet what a job I had! I never stopped adjusting the jibsheets at one side or the other, and with the wind varying like that I really had my hands full.

Next day was fine but the wind was light, from the south-west, and I had to keep tacking. Progress up the Sound was very slow. I was making for Oyster Bay, right at the other end of Long Island and not far from the entrance to the East River. I had already been two nights without sleep and could hardly keep my eyes open. At one moment I even dropped off for a minute or two, and jerked awake again just in time to go on the other tack, nearing the shore. In this narrow arm of the sea, that sort of thing could be dangerous. To ensure not falling asleep for good, I set my alarm clock to go off every half hour. That night was a long one.

The wind freshened a little next day and veered to the west, which enabled me to moor in Oyster Bay late that afternoon. In any case I should not have risked another sleepless night, but moored at some place on the way. It was twenty-two days since I had left Horta. If I had made for Newport I should have arrived two days sooner.

My crew joined me a few days later, and at Oyster Bay we had the use of the finest yacht club I know. Pen Duick II had been given her handicap by the American measurement, and we prepared for the races.

The first was on June 12 1966, Oyster Bay to Newport, a preliminary to the Bermuda race. There were not many entries, but the quality made up for the lack of numbers. In particular, there was the famous Ticonderoga, a large boat and the east coast champion of the Cal 40s, a class which had been successful in very many races. There was a headwind blowing, a thirty five knot nor'easter. It held from start to finish, and the boat sailed very well under jibs and mizzen, no mainsail, and we won that race.

The Newport to Bermuda was a much more serious affair. It is one of the classic ocean races, the Fastnet race being of course the queen of them all – because a boat is more likely to be tested on all points of sailing over this out-and-back course (Cowes-Fastnet-Plymouth) and because of the international entry. The best boats and crews of many countries take part, making the Fastnet race a real championship. The other major event, in addition to the Newport to Bermuda race, is the Sydney to Hobart. All three are over a distance of more than six hundred miles.

The entries for the Bermuda race were in five classes according to handicap. We were in class C. The largest boats were class A and the smallest class E. Each class started separately, beginning with class A, so we were able to watch the magnificent spectacle of a score of boats of more than sixty feet crowding to cross the line when the starting-gun went. Seven of them were 73-footers, the maximum length allowed, and from among these would come the real winner of the race, the boat to make the fastest actual time.

We had a bit of a breeze at the start, but this soon fell away and despite the amount of canvas we crowded on we weren't making much progress. Pen Duick II was definitely not a boat for light airs. Fortunately, these conditions did not last for long.

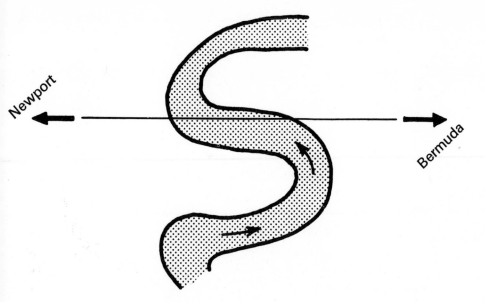

Newport

Bermuda

An important element in this race is the crossing of the Gulf Stream. Although its general direction is known, it meanders about and is subject to wind and weather, shifting unpredictably. American hydrographers who have been plotting the current's movements for some years are still unable to give an accurate long range forecast of its position. As can be seen from the sketch (9) this current can help or hinder a sailing vessel, depending on the point of approach. The importance of this will be readily understood when one realises that the main current of the Gulf Stream sometimes flows at four knots.

The problem is to know whether one is in a favourable stream or not. The only way of finding out is to take the temperature of the water before and after a change of course. The water is warmest in the main current. When the highest temperature has been taken, one alters course and by noticing the changes in temperature one can conclude whether the flow of current is favourable or not and whether there is any advantage in remaining in it.

However, the problem had been partly solved for us the day before the start of the race, when at the usual briefing a hydrographer had told us that the current had not shifted for several days and that when we reached the area in three days' time there was a strong possibility of it still not having varied. And indeed we did meet with a favourable branch of the current, just as forecast, almost on our direct route.

So there was no difficulty in that respect. On the other hand, we did run into violent storms and meet heavy seas, as often happens in this

9 Crossing the Gulf Stream

area of the Gulf Stream. The storms result from the mass of warm air coming from the Gulf Stream meeting colder air from chillier waters such as the Labrador Current. During the squalls, the strong wind increased even more and we had to keep trimming the sails or reducing canvas. We hugged the wind as much as possible, still maintaining speed, and on a course slightly to leeward of Bermuda. We were doing so well, despite the steep sea, that the aircraft keeping track of the race placed us easily first on handicap, until twenty-four hours before the finish. Throughout the rough weather we had kept to windward to better effect than any of the others and were well ahead – at least, so we were told on arrival at Hamilton. Unfortunately, the day before, the wind had unexpectedly swung round 45 degrees and we lost all our lead. We did no more than finish creditably, fifth in our class.

We were a bit disappointed, not to say vexed. It wasn't so much losing the handicap race, for to my mind that has little value. Trying to give a variety of craft of different sizes an even chance doesn't make sense, despite the time allowance, for the competitors are scattered about the ocean on different points of sailing in a long race and do not generally meet with the same wind and weather conditions. What vexed me was not to have finished first in our own class, the only worthwhile result.

I was consoled by the thought of making up for our defeat by a winning performance in the Bermuda to Copenhagen race, for which strong following winds are the rule and therefore just right for Pen Duick II. But obviously the 1966 season was not meant to be a lucky one for us. On the fourth day of the race we broke our tiller. The weather was fine and we were streaming along with a good wind on the quarter, carrying a spinnaker at each mast. I was at the tiller at the time, but very little effort was needed to keep the boat steady. Suddenly I felt the tiller go slack, and the boat started to broach. The spindle had broken. Yet it had already taken much greater strain; no doubt the metal was worn. I rigged up a makeshift tiller with a spi boom and some floorboards from the bottom of the cabin, the whole making a sort of long steering oar (10). It was a tiring contraption to handle, but it worked – except that if the boat was making more than five knots we could not keep her steady. So we were obliged to abandon, and we set course for St Pierre-et-Miquelon, making slow progress. Then we ran into fog and it stayed with us for five days, all the way to our destination.

I had no chart of the area with me, as this call was not in our programme, so finding the harbour in nil visibility was not easy. I drew a diagram – working from a chart of Belle Ile, which is on the same

latitude and so gave me the grid and the scale – and plotted the positions of the beacons and lighthouses as given in my nautical almanac. This gave me some idea of the channel and the navigational aids. We could hear the fog warnings and were getting radio bearings. I took in most of the canvas and we felt our way slowly, on tiptoe so to speak, listening to the foghorns and the waves breaking on the rocks and keeping the lead going. So we eventually got into St Pierre, where no one could do enough for us. A new tiller was fitted, and after five days – three of them still foggy – we set sail again in a mist that you could have cut with a knife. We had to steer by compass to get out of harbour, and the thick mist stayed with us for another five long days.

However, the Atlantic crossing was made under spinnakers nearly all the time, and we reached Granville without incident.

10   Philippe Lavat and Michel Vanek struggling to steer with the jury tiller

2

Six wins for
Pen Duick III

Before leaving for the United states I had completed the design of Pen Duick III and handed it over to the La Perrière boatyard at Lorient for the construction plan to be drawn up. This new boat was going to be built of aluminium alloy (Duralinox), which was the reason for my changing boatbuilder, as the Constantini brothers at La Trinité (who

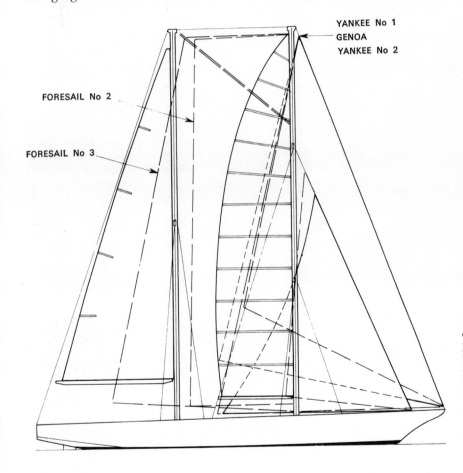

YANKEE No 1
GENOA
YANKEE No 2

FORESAIL No 2

FORESAIL No 3

11   Pen Duick III
original rig
Mainsail: 342 sq ft
No 2 Foresail: 674 sq ft
No 3 Foresail: 1005 sq ft
Genoa: 860 sq ft
No 1 Yankee: 714 sq ft
No 2 Yankee: 571 sq ft
Genoa jib: 408 sq ft
No 1 jib: 275 sq ft

15

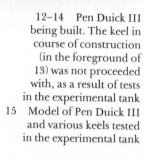

12–14   Pen Duick III
being built. The keel in
course of construction
(in the foreground of
13) was not proceeded
with, as a result of tests
in the experimental tank
15   Model of Pen Duick III
and various keels tested
in the experimental tank

had built Pen Duick II) built only of timber. On my return to France I went to Lorient; the weight estimate had just been made, and we considered it in relation to the design. Only a few very minor modifications were needed, which made practically no difference to the lines of the boat. We then carried out tests with a model of the hull in an experimental tank at Nantes, comparing its qualities with a model of Pen Duick II.

My chief aim in designing Pen Duick III had been – while keeping a sense of proportion – to obtain a better handicap rating than with Pen Duick II. I had had my first experience of English and American measurement formulae with the latter boat, and I was seeking to avoid some of the mistakes I had made in this respect. I was also aiming at a faster boat – again, keeping a sense of proportion. As Pen Duick III would be much the bigger boat, with a waterline length of 42 feet 3 inches as against 32 feet 6 inches, she would naturally be the faster, but I wanted to obtain an increase in speed in addition to that due to the greater length. This is what I was trying to determine by testing a model in the experimental tank. The tests showed that the aim had been achieved, so I decided to leave well alone and not to modify the design any further. We also experimented with models of differing keels (15) while having the use of the experimental tank, and decided which would be the best.

Pen Duick III was launched at Lorient at the beginning of May 1967. There was just a week in which to try her out at sea, where she performed satisfactorily, and then it was time to sail for St Malo where we were to compete to represent France in the Admiral's Cup. This international competition is held every other year, and each country enters three boats rating between twenty-five and seventy feet. The result is determined by the total number of points won by the three boats in four of the season's races – the Channel Race, the Fastnet, and two of those held during Cowes Week.

My crew, except for the three who sailed with me from Lorient, were new to the boat. I was a little anxious, for although they made a good crew they needed more practise in sailing a big boat like Pen Duick III. We won the first race at Cowes – narrowly, and after several muddles, notably with the spinnaker. We won the second more easily, our handling of the boat having greatly improved. Fortunately a good crew soon get used to a boat.

Then, in early June, came the Morgan Cup, the RORC's first important race of the season, over a triangular course starting and finishing at Portsmouth; the first leg is to round a buoy off Cherbourg, then to the Royal Sovereign lightvessel, and so home to Portsmouth. We won this

16 Pen Duick III
Length overall: 57 ft
Length waterline: 42 ft 3 in
Beam: 13 ft 8 in
Draft: 8 ft 10 in
Displacement: 13½ tons
Builder: La Perrière, Lorient

race by a comfortable margin, but luck was with us. After rounding the
buoy, instead of setting course for the Royal Sovereign, which meant
tacking into a north-east wind, I preferred to tack along the French
coast and then head across the Channel. I think I thereby had more

favourable currents than the other competitors, but in addition – which was where the luck came in – I had a more favourable wind.

We then sailed to Sweden to compete in the round-Gotland race, to be held in early June. We passed through the Kiel Canal by 'thumbing a lift' from barges, which took us in tow. Then we made for Sandham at an average of nearly nine knots. Sandham, in the archipelago between Lake Maelar and the Baltic at Stockholm, is one of Sweden's chief yachting venues. It has a splendid club and the whole archipelago is magnificent. Several old friends were already there, among them Anahita in which I had sailed to Sweden in September 1965, and that amazing boat Britt-Marie and her congenial owners. Britt-Marie was one of the Skerry Cruiser class, 65 feet long, 7 feet 6 inches in the beam, ten tons displacement, and she now had a sail area of 1,300 square feet.

The race started from Sandham on July 4 – an out-and-back course, after rounding the island of Gotland. There was only a light wind, as is often the case in the Baltic, and we were close hauled on the outward leg and had a following wind for the homeward, but it freshened only towards the end. We were in the lead all the way until halfway back, when Germania, a 70-footer, overhauled us. However, we easily won the handicap race.

We cruised among the islands for a while, before returning to England for the Channel Race. A Swedish friend invited us to his island, and we sailed there in his wake. Then we called at Oland, a Finnish

17 Looking down on Pen Duick III from the maintop

island, and went over the four-masted, square-rigger Pommern, now laid up and no more than a memory of the fleet of Cape Horners run by Gustaf Erikson. This Oland shipowner was the last to run big square-riggers on a commercial basis, sending them to Australia to load wheat during the years between the two World Wars. From Oland we sailed to Helsinki, and by then it was high time to turn south. On the way, we put in at Copenhagen, then barge-hitched through the Kiel Canal again. It had been a wonderful cruise, we all agreed, and we looked forward to spending a longer time in the Baltic another year.

The Channel Race was on August 2. Like the Morgan Cup, it is held over a triangular course from Portsmouth – round the Royal Sovereign lightvessel, round the lightship off Le Havre and home to Portsmouth and the finishing line. We had following winds nearly all the way to the Le Havre lightship, then the breeze eased. It was another win for us.

At the start of the Fastnet on August 10 there was only a very slight wind, and we were close hauled all the way down Channel; the wind freshened a little but the sea was still too flat for Pen Duick III to show her paces. Then the wind backed to the south, we set the spinnaker and were soon running before a quartering wind and steering for the Fastnet light, off the south coast of Ireland. We rounded the lighthouse astern of the big Gitana but ahead of the American Figaro and the German Rubin – though these two were ahead of us on corrected time. 18 The Fastnet Race But we increased our lead on the homeward leg, beating into a

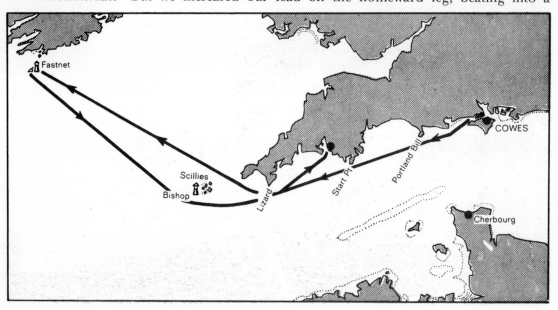

boisterous south-south-east wind. It was dead on our nose as we came up to the Bishop Rock. The wind strength and direction were very variable on the homeward leg, for there were storms about. The other boats were generally on the starboard tack, apparently expecting the wind to back. I preferred to keep changing tack each time the wind shifted, and these tactics favoured us. Moreover, the boat was performing very well in the rather confused sea and strong wind, and we crossed the finishing line with a good lead over the others.

Our last two races of the season were Plymouth to La Rochelle and La Rochelle to Bénodet. There was a moderate breeze for the start of the Plymouth race. The Italian Levantades was in the lead crossing the Channel, then the wind hardened and, close hauled, we took the lead from her. We ran into very rough weather soon afterwards, the worst of the season without a doubt. We rounded Ushant in a sou'west gale and with rough seas, conditions not to be wondered at in that area, and as they held until La Rochelle we came into our own and registered our fifth win of the season. The sixth was gained in the La Rochelle to Bénodet race, close hauled in a moderate breeze.

3
The Sydney
to Hobart race

This successful season made us decide to enter for the Sydney to Hobart race, held on December 26 – a time of year much more suitable for ocean racing in Australian waters than in north European. In the weeks before leaving I began preliminary work on a new idea: despite Pen Duick III's great qualities, my mind was turning more and more to a multihulled boat for the next Transatlantic race. But the money had to be found first, for the designing and researching of such a boat are expensive.

In November I sailed Pen Duick III to La Pallice and saw her put aboard the Vanoise, bound for Sydney. A month later I flew out with two of my crew, Yves Guégan and Olivier de Kersauson, to be in Sydney when the cargo ship arrived. The other members of the crew had been unable to get away in time, but were to follow us a few days later. In the event, they reached Sydney on the day Pen Duick III was being unloaded, as the Vanoise had been held up in another Australian port by a dock strike. So with a full crew to hoist the rigging, Pen Duick III was put afloat again that same evening for us by the club organizing the race. The few days before the start were fully occupied with preparations and the various controls. The racing rules of the Cruising Club of Australia are not the same as those of the RORC. Before leaving France, Pen Duick III had been fitted with a Renault engine; this now had to be started and run in the presence of the race organizers, as each entry must have an engine in working order for use in an emergency.

The starting line was in the harbour, and I could see that in order to reach the open sea we should have to manoeuvre, or rather thread our way, between the other competitors and the swarm of spectators' craft. This race was obviously a great event for Australians, and it seemed as if everything that could float was milling about the harbour, packed to the gunwales. People who had not been able to get a place in a boat were gathered on the cliffs at the harbour entrance for a view of the scene.

The gun went and we crossed the line with a south-east wind on our backs (19). We were in among a cluster of boats that were taking our wind, and we couldn't draw clear. The competitors nearer land were favoured with a stronger wind and began to draw ahead. Before leaving the harbour, we all had to round a buoy. As we were taking in the spinnaker, having already hauled down the big foresail, I noticed a certain amount of indecision among the leading boats. They could not find the buoy in the position where it ought to have been, and were in doubt as to what to do.

We looked for it too. The craft filled with spectators added to the confusion. A motor launch scraped against our starboard bow, then swung wildly round and ran down a dinghy without hesitation, leaving the three occupants floundering. We did not linger to help rescue them, for someone had sighted the missing buoy far to leeward. The whole fleet of competitors streaked towards it (20). The leaders had the wind taken from them by the boats coming up and overhauling them, so that we all reached the buoy in a bunch, eight or ten abreast. The boats nearest the buoy had difficulty in enforcing their right to round it, the others no less in edging aside their neighbours. We were on the inside, and I was not displeased at having a good, strong, metal hull, an excellent argument in such a situation for maintaining one's rights. There was a certain amount of splintering and grinding; one boat was sandwiched between us and the one astern, but eventually we were all round the buoy, Pen Duick III being fourth. We heard later that the buoy had broken adrift. In all that congestion only one boat suffered serious damage, her backstay having been torn away by someone's stem, and she was obliged to retire.

We were sailing close hauled and on an easterly course as we reached the open sea. The question then was whether to continue on this tack and stand out to sea before changing course to the south or to turn south at once. According to the weather forecast, the south-east wind would not hold for long but would back to the north-east, which is the prevailing wind at that time of year. However, I had heard all the local yachtsmen say that the north-east wind fell right away during the night; there was then a flat calm offshore, but apparently a light wind could be found out to sea. I tried to avoid the flat calm by standing out to sea. Many boats headed south, but I noticed that our chief rivals were adopting the same tactics as we were. For a while we were the leading boat of this group, then the New Zealand Kahurangui overhauled us. She was a splendid 65-footer and made a brave sight sailing close hauled in the slightly choppy sea. Another New Zealand 65-footer, Fidelis, was to leeward of us but we were drawing away from

19 The start of the
Sydney to Hobart race

20 Pen Duick III in
Sydney Harbour. The
spinnaker has broken
away from the boom

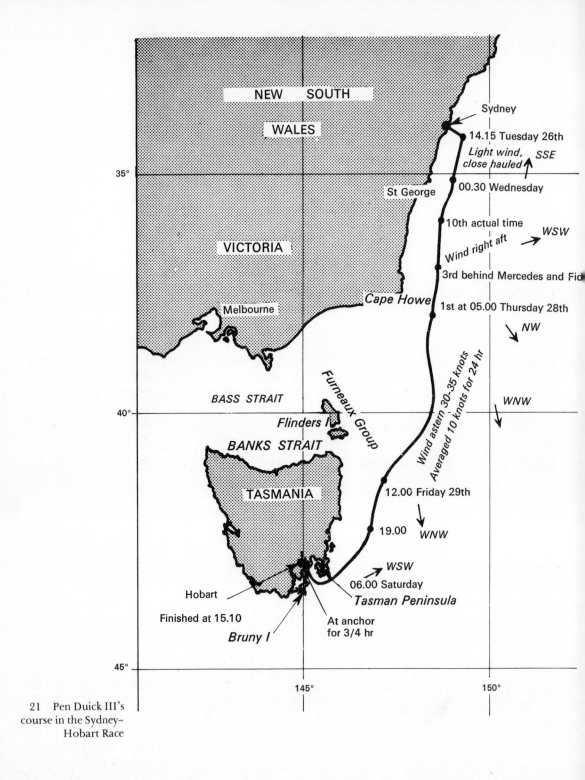

NEW SOUTH

WALES

Sydney

14.15 Tuesday 26th

Light wind, *SSE*
close hauled

35°

St George

00.30 Wednesday

10th actual time

WSW

VICTORIA

Wind right aft

3rd behind Mercedes and Fid

Cape Howe

1st at 05.00 Thursday 28th

Melbourne

NW

Wind astern 30-35 knots
Averaged 10 knots for 24 hr

BASS STRAIT

Furneaux Group

WNW

40°

Flinders I

BANKS STRAIT

TASMANIA

12.00 Friday 29th

WNW

19.00

WSW

Hobart

06.00 Saturday

Finished at 15.10

Tasman Peninsula

At anchor
for 3/4 hr

Bruny I

45°

145°

150°

21 Pen Duick III's
course in the Sydney–
Hobart Race

her. We kept on this tack for six miles, then changed course to the south.

During the evening the wind fell away as predicted, and there was a flat calm all night. We had not avoided it after all, and our board to the east was so much time lost. The north-east wind rose in the morning and spinnakers were set on all the boats. It would take all day to come up with the competitors who had headed south immediately on leaving Sydney harbour. Some of them were small boats, and to beat them on handicap we needed to be well ahead of them.

Fidelis had passed us while the wind was light, but when the breeze had taken a firm hold we began to match her speed. Then the wind backed to the north and we had it right aft. Kahurangui was well astern of us. The wind backed further during the night, and the following morning, Thursday, none of our rivals was in sight.

The race regulations required us to carry a radio transmitter (I had rented ours while in Sydney) and to report our position twice a day. At the same time we heard the positions of the other competitors, and so we learnt that we were in the lead that morning. And we kept increasing it. When on the level of Bass Strait, the north-wester strengthened so much that we had to change the large spinnaker for a smaller one and to take in the mainsail. We ran before this strong wind down to the Tasman Peninsula, at the head of the large bay into which the Hobart river flows. But then the wind eased and almost died, so that we were soon on short tacks, searching for wind to make westing. And yet this bay is called Storm! There was not a breath of wind as we came to the estuary; and the tide was ebbing, so we had to anchor. There we remained for almost an hour, then got under way again, still tacking and making slow progress. The last forty miles, from the Tasman Peninsula to Hobart, were covered at an average of three knots.

We crossed the finishing line in the late afternoon to the cheers of the crowds packing the quays. Australians take a keen interest in this race, which is why competitors are required to radio their positions twice a day. The public expects newspapers and radio stations to keep it informed of the progress of the race.

The second and third boats to finish were Fidelis and Kahurangui. We quickly learnt that we were first of our class, and by a good margin, and to me that was what mattered. But to the Australians, what mattered most was the result of the handicap race. This seemed illogical to me. When Rainbow crossed the finishing line we heard that this class III boat had beaten us by a few minutes on corrected time. A handicap race would only have some meaning if the wind remained

22　Pen Duick III on a
reach

23　A wall of canvas –
Pen Duick III close
reaching

constant, which hardly ever happens. In an ocean race the distance between the small and the large boats is so great thay they do not race with the same wind conditions. Therefore the result is distorted, and the handicap result becomes a matter of luck.

24 In a strong breeze, under mainsail and small spinnaker
25 Pen Duick III with the wind abeam

We had won in our own class in all of the six European races, but on only three occasions had we also won the handicap race (including the two classics, the Fastnet and the Channel Race), and that was because each time the winds had favoured the big boats. In fact it is unusual for a class II boat to win the handicap race. The Sydney to Hobart is a good example. When we had rounded the Tasman Peninsula, Rainbow was seventy miles behind us – a considerable distance – and if we had covered the final forty miles at a normal speed or even a little slower, which ought to have enabled us to hold on to our seventy mile lead, the Rainbow would have had to complete the course at an average of a little more than ten knots in order to beat us on handicap, as we were giving her seven hours. Now that sort of average speed over a distance is practically beyond the capabilities of a boat of Rainbow's size. So in theory we could not be beaten – all the Australian press were agreed. But exceptional circumstances reversed the situation. While we were creeping towards the finish, Rainbow was streaming along at maximum speed with a good favourable wind, and she was able to maintain

26　Eric Tabarly (centre, front row) and the crew of Pen Duick III

this speed across Storm Bay, where the wind had risen again. It was a situation which made any comparison impossible; and in such conditions a handicap race makes no sense.

This was the last time Pen Duick III was raced with her schooner rig. The RORC now considered that the manner of measuring the sail area of a schooner was too favourable, and had decided to revise the rules as from January 1, 1968. The committee had not done things by halves: henceforth a schooner had no chance of finishing in the first three, let alone of winning, so severely was this rig penalized.

So I decided to give Pen Duick III a ketch rig if I entered her for any more races. It seemed to me that she would have just as good a chance with that rig, for our seven successes in seven races were not due only to her schooner rig. They were also due to the hull, a speedy hull specially designed to be given a relatively low handicap; and they were due to her crew. The best number for sailing Pen Duick III is nine. The crew were not always quite the same for these races, so that altogether the following fourteen were in the crew at one time or another: Pierre English, Pierre Fouquin, Jean-Pierre Fournier, Daniel Gilles, Yves Guégan, Olivier de Kersauson, Philippe Lavat, Bernard Le Roi, Gérard Petitpas, Jean-Jacques Sévi, Guy Tabarly, Patrick Tabarly, Yves Troadec and Michel Vanek. They are all very good seamen and most of them had sailed with me on Pen Duick II; a few had even been with me on the first Pen Duick. They have all known one another for years and consequently get on well together. So I always had a first-rate crew.

Gérard Petitpas navigated the boat, and I knew I could leave that side of things in his very capable hands and devote much more time myself to the handling and trimming of the sails and to the tactics of a race. Only one tactical mistake was made that season, I think – when we tacked out to sea at the start of the Sydney to Hobart race. Even that was not disastrous, as all the best boats did the same.

Most of the crew had to return to France after the race, and only Olivier de Kersauson, Pierre English and Yves Guégan were able to stay on with me. Alain Colas, French professor at Sydney University, joined us for a cruise to New Caledonia (27) before returning to Sydney. He had been one of Kahurangui's crew for the race, and we were taking him back. We had a month to spare, as Pen Duick III was not due to be shipped back to France until the beginning of February.

We sailed from Hobart on January 2. A fortnight later we had a new and alarming experience when we ran into a small cyclone. We were returning to Noumea from Ouvea, one of the small islands of the Loyalty group, and were on a south-west course with a Force 6 wind on our port beam. Suddenly we found ourselves getting too close to the coral reef – in that steep sea it was impossible to see the breakers until quite near, and poor visibility was shutting out the land. We turned away, and I hoisted the mainsail with two reefs in it as we went on the starboard tack. Just then the wind veered and hardened, shifting from south-east to south-west in a very short time. We took in the jib. Torrential rain poured down and the wind was blowing at more than seventy miles an hour. Under reduced sail, close hauled, we were making eight knots. What with the streaming rain and the sheets of spray being whipped up by the wind or flung back from the stem there was so much moisture in the air that at times it was difficult to breathe. Looking to windward became impossible with that avalanche of water flying in our faces. The sea was a foaming whiteness with clouds of spray sent whirling skywards by the shrieking wind, which was still increasing in strength. I was at the helm and suddenly saw two adjacent seams give way near the foot of the mainsail. I gave the order to take in the mainsail, but before the crew could free the halyard winch some more seams had given way. The strain on the boltrope was so great that it broke away and the sail ripped across about 18 inches above the boom. This left the upper part of the sail streaming from the mast at the end of the halyard. One would have thought this large amount of canvas streaming from the mast would jerk and shake the rigging; but so strong was the wind that it stood out as stiff as a plank and was not even flapping. However, it was dangerous, and I had the halyard cut away near the foot of the mast. But nothing happened – the halyard must have been dragged from its block and caught up on something. About an hour later, however, the whole lot was whisked away.

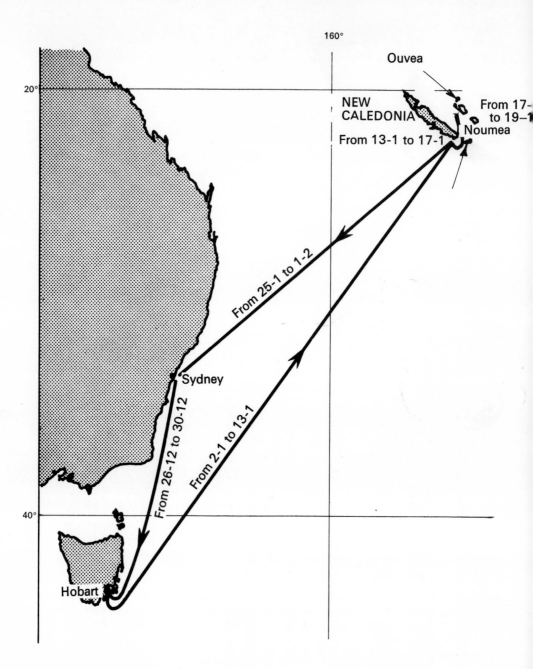

160°

Ouvea

20°

NEW
CALEDONIA

From 17-
to 19-1

Noumea

From 13-1 to 17-1

From 25-1 to 1-2

Sydney

From 26-12 to 30-12

From 2-1 to 13-1

40°

Hobart

27   A cruise to New
        Caledonia

Meanwhile we were still close hauled with only the small jib set. The wind was blowing at what must have been hurricane force, and despite the reduced canvas we were heeling more sharply than ever before. We were still making seven and a half knots in this big sea. None of us had ever known such a gale of wind (we learnt later, from the weather men at Noumea, that in the area where we were – almost in the path of the cyclone – there had been winds of about one hundred miles an hour), and at moments like that one appreciates having good strong sails. If we had been close to land, our lives and our boat would have depended upon the jib's resistance, for the boat had shown that even in these weather conditions she could still sail well to windward. Fortunately we were not in that dangerous situation, and I thought it was senseless to continue close hauled when there was no question in such weather of seeking a channel through the reefs to Noumea. The sail and rigging were having strains put on them to no purpose. The jib might be torn away at any moment, and I thought it was quite enough to have lost a mainsail. So we decided to take in the jib. It was quite an effort to go forward in the face of that wind; there was a short struggle to master the flapping canvas, and then all was suddenly peaceful.

It was unbelievable – the moment we were under bare poles we no longer felt the effects of the big sea. A few moments earlier the boat had been heeled sharply and was being tossed about violently, the flying spray coming abroad, and now we were lying quietly with the wind abeam, well balanced and – due to her minimum underwater area – sliding to leeward at quite a rate. Her wake was flattening the sea a little, and with that leeway she was avoiding the violence of the waves. The wind pressure on the bare rigging was heeling her slightly, so that she was not rolling very much – in fact there was just a gentle roll. As we had plenty of sea room to drift to leeward, we could now go below and wait for the weather to improve. Just before midnight the wind dropped as quickly as it had risen. We made sail and got under way close hauled. Six hours had passed since taking in all the canvas.

Without a mainsail we could not set any canvas to the mainmast, so Pen Duick III found herself converted to a cutter. In the morning, when in sight of land, I reckoned from our position that the previous night we must have been drifting at about three and a half knots. This was enormous, and explained why we had been riding easily under bare poles. The waters were strewn with branches and vegetation, which gave a rather sinister impression.

However, the experience had assured me that Pen Duick III behaved remarkably well under bare poles; and I now knew that in winds of that strength we needed to have a combination of small, very strong sails on board.

A few days later we sailed from Noumea bound for Sydney, where Pen Duick III was to be shipped to France aboard the Vanoise.

4

Pen Duick IV — multihull

On my return to France I went to the La Perrière boatyard at Lorient, which was building a trimaran (28) for me. Work on it had begun several months previously. Early in September I had gone to Sète, on the Mediterranean, to see the architect André Allègre. Recent experiences and the news circulating about the entries for the coming Transatlantic race had convinced me that it would be won by a multihulled boat. I preferred a trimaran as being safer than a catamaran, which tends to capsize more easily. André Allègre agreed with me, and as he is a specialist in this kind of boat I had asked him to collaborate with me in designing a 65 foot trimaran.

We had thought of having one symmetrical hull and two assymetrical, as the latter develop a lift which makes them less inclined to skid to leeward. Many multihulled boats, especially catamarans, have flat or almost flat outer sides to the hulls for this reason. In our case, however, we intended to have a centreboard in the middle hull. We tested various models in the experimental tank to find the best shape and combination, and finally decided that all the hulls should be symmetrical.

However, further work on the design of the boat had been held up for lack of money, and it was not until just before I left for Australia that the building of the boat had begun. Good progress had been made during my absence. The construction plan was the work of Monsieur Joseph Rouillard of Nantes, a guarantee in itself. The structural qualities of a trimaran are all-important; the stress and strain on certain parts, such as the struts joining the floats to the hull are considerable; they need to be strong, yet not heavy, for it is essential to keep down the weight of this kind of boat by all possible means.

Unfortunately we began to fall behind with the building programme, and a ban on overtime by the boatyard workers did not help matters. The time I had allowed for the boat's trials – which was not long – was growing shorter, and this had me worried. In the end, Pen

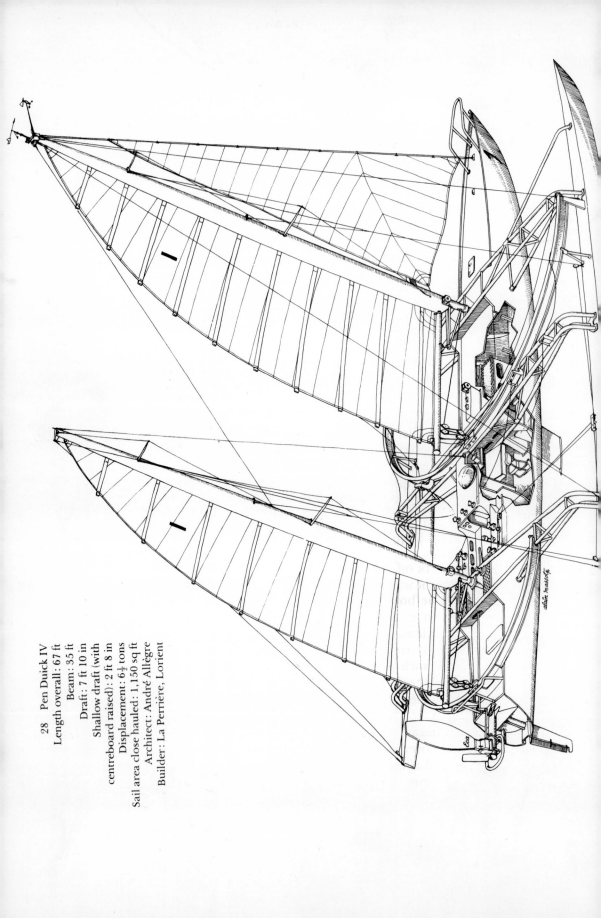

28   Pen Duick IV
Length overall: 67 ft
Beam: 35 ft
Draft: 7 ft 10 in
Shallow draft (with
centreboard raised): 2 ft 8 in
Displacement: 6½ tons
Sail area close hauled: 1,150 sq ft
Architect: André Allègre
Builder: La Perrière, Lorient

Duick IV was not launched (29) until May 11. She was still not quite
ready for sailing, and her first trials were due to be held on May 14. A
week later I should have to leave for Plymouth and the start of the
Transatlantic race.

There was only a light wind for her first trials, and I had shipped the
spare rudder as the proper one was not ready. Tacking in Lorient
roads showed her ability to turn was quite good for a trimaran. Then
we left the roadstead, and as we reached open water the wind freshened
a little. Suddenly I noticed the masts bending alarmingly. I had no
wish to risk them breaking so soon, and I took in all the canvas and got
a tow back. It was all very worrying – would the lower shrouds due to
be added next day keep the mast straight? Apparently not, for the next
time we went out we did not get much farther than on the previous
occasion before I had to have the sails hauled down again. More time
was lost in fitting runners. Then the mast was secure, but going about
became a complicated manoeuvre! When tacking out at sea it is very
important for the runners to be adjusted in time, otherwise the mast
might break. The moment to do this is when the mast is just about
straight in the fore and aft direction, that is to say when dead into the
eye of the wind. Then one runner has to be tightened and the other
eased off at once, otherwise it would prevent the mast from inclining to
leeward.

At last the boat was all in order, and she proved to be a very fast
sailer. That was all to the good; but then the self-steering gear, which
had only just been installed, caused me some concern. It acted
perfectly when moving slowly, but when the boat was moving fast its
fierceness made me anxious. We tried to improve its action, but time
was against us as usual and a satisfactory solution had still not been
reached when I sailed to La Trinité. Pen Duick III was lying there, and
I wanted to compare the two boats. Sailing Pen Duick IV singlehanded
against Pen Duick III with a full crew, I easily beat her on all points of
sailing. This naturally convinced me even more that the trimaran was
the right boat for the Transatlantic race. Nevertheless, if I could still
have made a choice I would have sailed Pen Duick III in the race, for
Pen Duick IV was obviously far from ready. There were too many
things liable to let me down. But the firm constructing the two
self-steering gears for the two boats had informed me, right at the last
minute, that it could not deliver both in time. It was one or the other,
and a decision had to be made. I felt so sure that Pen Duick IV, despite
not then being ready for sailing, would be faster then Pen Duick III
that I had ordered her self-steering gear to be completed. So Pen
Duick III remained behind at Lorient and I sailed Pen Duick IV to

29   Pen Duick IV at her
launching
30   At Plymouth,
before the start of the
Transatlantic race

Plymouth (30) telling myself that I should be very lucky to reach the finish of the race.

I did not in fact get very far. The first accident occurred during the first night at sea, but it had nothing to do with the boat's lack of readiness. The shipping lanes off the south-west coast of England are always very busy and I had to stay on deck all night to avoid being run down by a cargo vessel. My navigation lights were far from being powerful, and might not be seen in time. There is a rule of the sea that steamers must give way to sailing craft, but before they can give way they do have to sight the sailing boat. At about midnight I was watching a ship on a collision course with me. Shortly afterwards I saw her change course slightly so that she would pass astern of me. But at the last minute she altered course again and was coming straight at me. I quickly tacked, and avoided her by no more than fifty or sixty feet. It had been a near thing! Later, around three in the morning, as there was no shipping in sight I went below to have some coffee. I had not been below fifteen minutes when a frightening bump sent me hurrying on deck. I saw the wide bows of a cargo vessel towering over me to starboard. The vessel was practically stopped, and my starboard float scraped along her bows before we were past. Pen Duick IV went sailing on and increased speed again. I took a torch and went to inspect the starboard float; until I knew what damage had been caused I couldn't be sure of being able to tack. There was a big gash along the forward part of the float, but it affected only the first compartment, which was tightly packed with foam rubber. So water could not get in there. The other compartments did not seem to have been touched, and I thought it was all right to carry on.

However, at midday a mizzen shroud broke, and this made it necessary to put back for repairs, as the mast was likely to come down. I put about, and then found I should have had to return to Plymouth in any case, as the second compartment of the starboard float had sprung a leak. Back at Plymouth the float was patched up for me by the Navy and the rigging was repaired at Mashford's yard. Thanks to everyone's speedy help, I was able to set off again only four days behind the other competitors.

This time I still did not get very far. The self-steering gear broke down and I could hardly work the rudder. I put into Newlyn, repaired the self-steering gear, and left again a day later. But a few miles out to sea the device broke down again. I put back to Newlyn, and this time I was finished with the race. Two friends, Pierre Fouquin and Victor Tonnerre, came across from France to help me sail the boat back to Lorient, which we did with some difficulty due to the loose rudder.

At Lorient we found that the rudder hangings had been loosened by the bump received from the cargo vessel, and it would not have held much longer. There was no good crying over spilt milk.

The La Perrière boatyard did the necessary repairs and I sailed again from Lorient to take part in the Crystal Trophy, a race for multihulls only, over a triangular course. We had a brisk west wind at the start; and during the night, when we were off the Glénans, the wind hardened considerably. We took in the mainsail, and were making good progress close hauled under jib and mizzen. But then, alas, the lever of the mizzen backstay on the weather side suddenly gave way, bringing down the mizzen mast. The mainmast seemed satisfied to bow deeply and remained that way. But it too would have come down if we had not already lowered the mainsail, for the backstays of both masts lead down to the same lever. We put back to Lorient under the jib. It seemed fated that I should never race with this boat.

However, there was still time to take part in the RORC's last two races of the season – the Yarmouth to Santander and the Santander to La Trinité – with Pen Duick III, which I converted into a ketch.

I had made provisions for this when she was being built, so the change-over was not complicated (31). I took out the mainmast and stepped a smaller mast on the cabin roof. The chainplates were already in place. This mast had been used for one of Pen Duick II's many conversions. Then all that remained to be done was to order the shrouds and the sails, and to install a horse for the new mainsheet.

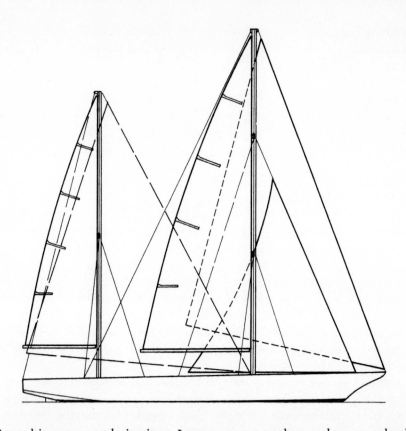

31 Pen Duick III
ketch rigged
Mainsail: 446 sq ft
Mizzen: 238 sq ft
Staysail: 698 sq ft
Headsails as before

Everything was ready in time. I got a crew together and we won both races. The season had not been a complete failure and I was happy enough with this successful ending, which confirmed my opinion of Pen Duick III – that even with a ketch rig she is a good boat. It does not improve her looks though, and she loses all the advantages of a schooner rig, undoubtedly the best of all rigs for ocean racing and for singlehanded races. In my opinion it is a great pity that a schooner rig suffered so badly in the recent revision of handicap rules. In any case, there would be no difficulty if I wished to convert Pen Duick III into a schooner again. With a crane, the masts and rigging can be changed in half a day.

Part Two

The Transpacific race:
basic problems

5
The boat
and the route

In the summer of 1968 I read in a yachting magazine that the Slocum Society was organizing a singlehanded Transpacific race. The start was to be on March 15 1969, from San Francisco Bay, and the finish was at the entrance to the bay of Tokyo. It was a race for single-hulled boats whose length overall was between twenty-two and thirty-five feet. I was greatly tempted to enter, for singlehanded races are few and far between, so one should take advantage of it when such a race is held. Moreover, this one was attractive because of its length, and there were already reports of fifteen probable competitors. In France alone, it seemed, the four of us who had taken part in singlehanded Trans-atlantic races were considering entering for this Transpacific race.

Unfortunately, I had no boat meeting the requirements of the race. So if I were going to enter I had to start thinking of building another Pen Duick. Was this reasonable? There were several matters to be taken into consideration. First, if I did not enter, I was unlikely to have another chance of taking part in a singlehanded race before the next Transatlantic, to be held in 1972 – which then meant in four years time! And I had heard that some of the intending competitors were already designing boats specially for the race. So that in any case the problem of building another Pen Duick would arise. Even if I had a single-hulled boat less than thirty-five feet in length, she would probably have been built with a different aim in mind and would not necessarily be the best possible boat for this Transpacific race.

Altogether I felt urged to find a solution to the problem, but without getting very far, I must admit. For one thing, I had no idea how to finance the building of a new boat. And even if I found the money, the time seemed very short to design and build the boat, carry out some trials and have her shipped to San Francisco by early March.

However, I made some enquiries and put out a feeler or two. I had become increasingly convinced, since my experiences with Pen Duick III and Pen Duick IV, of the advantages of Duralinox – aluminium alloy – for the construction of racing yachts. So I asked the La Perrière boatyard at Lorient, the builders of those two boats, if they could build a Pen Duick V, overall length thirty-five feet, for delivery by Christmas. They said it was possible, provided the construction plan was ready by mid October – which meant that the architect's design had to be in their hands before the end of September. This left very little time, so little that I should have to forego the testing of models in an experimental tank; which was a pity. Never mind – the unexpected would play a still greater part. It was a risk that had to be taken.

I still had to find an architect, and I thought of Dick Carter, whose qualities as a sailor and yachtsman I admire as much as his abilities as a boat designer. Perhaps my project would interest him. At La Trinité, I asked Vanek – who manages the sale of Dick's boats in France – to put the proposition to him. He sent a favourable reply. But in the meantime, while at the Mediterranean International Boat Week, I was introduced to Michel Bigoin by my friend Pierre Fouquin, who had recently begun working as an engineer for the La Perriére boatyard. I already knew of Bigoin's work as an architect and had seen at least two of his boats – Samourai, a class IV boat, brand new, which had just covered herself with glory at the regatta held in conjunction with the Boat Week, and Flying Forty, a boat that was several years old but very speedy, particularly good at planing with a following wind.

I explained what I wanted to do, and Michel Bigoin at once showed great interest. I decided there and then to entrust him with designing Pen Duick V, not only because I had confidence in him but because I thought I could save time by having a French architect. I have, after all, some notions about designing a boat and I wanted to discuss the matter with the architect. By meeting him and talking it over, instead of by corresponding with one working abroad, valuable time would obviously be saved.

Michel Bigoin told me that he and his partner, Daniel Duvergie, could get down to work on the boat straight away, and they thought they could have the design ready for my approval in a fortnight or so. I gave him the following directives: an overall length of thirty-five feet, to obtain all possible advantage from the rules of the race, and a boat that was very fast with a following wind, was capable of planing over the water, and could also perform well when close hauled. It was a simple enough programme – to design a boat which would sail very fast all the time. Fortunately the architects had no need to worry about measurement formulae, as there was no handicap race.

The reason why I wanted a boat which was particularly fast with a following wind resulted from studying the route and the wind systems in the pacific.

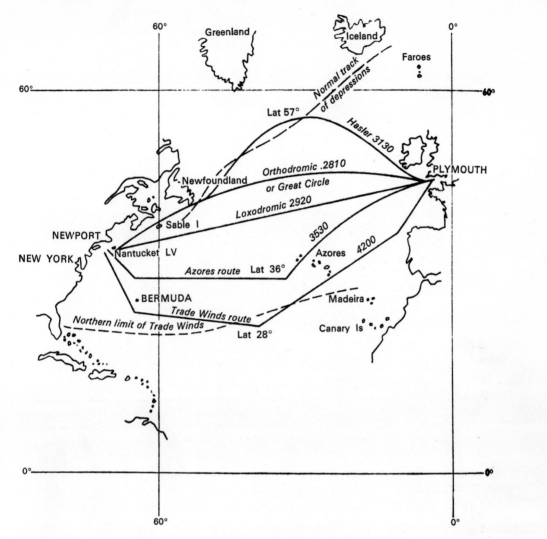

The same question arose as for the Transatlantic singlehanded race – whether to choose the shortest route in distance or the route likely to benefit most from favourable winds. My choice of route in the Transatlantic race (32) had not been easy to make, for the shortest route – the Orthodromic or Great Circle – did not appear to have much advantage over the more southerly routes; it was three or four days faster than the latter at most, which was not to be disdained yet was, after all, largely theoretical. For the Transpacific race, however, the choice was much simpler (33).

32 Possible routes across the Atlantic

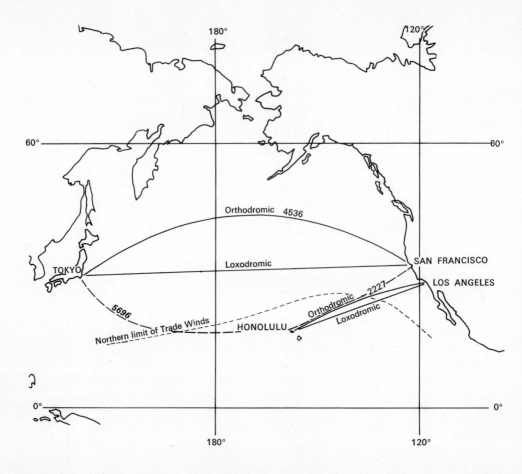

Orthodromic 4536

Loxodromic

SAN FRANCISCO

LOS ANGELES

TOKYO

5696

Orthodromic 2227

Loxodromic

Northern limit of Trade Winds

HONOLULU

33 Possible routes across the Pacific

The average wind conditions in the two oceans are very similar, though. On the same latitude and at the same time of year the conditions have very much in common. As in the North Atlantic, the prevailing winds in the North Pacific are the westerlies; and like the tropical zone of the Atlantic, that of the Pacific benefits from the Trade Winds. In each ocean variables are found between these two wind systems. Why then, with so similar conditions prevailing should the choice of route be narrower for the Transpacific race?

In the first place, the date was different. The start of the 1964 Transatlantic race had been May 23, whereas this Transpacific race was to start on March 15. Consequently winter would hardly be over and westerly storms would still be fairly frequent in the North Pacific. The percentage of westerly winds indicated on the pilot charts is extremely high, and have an average strength of Force 5. The Great Circle route – the shortest – would take me through areas where for ten per cent of the time these winds reach Force 8 – blowing at more than forty miles an hour. This means, in nautical terms, a fresh gale, the sea rough and disturbed, with waves twenty to twenty-five feet high. In conditions of that nature, sailing a small boat no more than thirty-five feet long is a severe test.

Secondly, the distance of the Transpacific race, San Francisco to Tokyo, was much longer than the race from Plymouth to Newport; so the more southerly route did not increase the distance, compared with that by the Great Circle, by so great a percentage. The shortest route between Plymouth and Newport – the Great Circle, which I had taken – is 2,810 miles. By taking the Azores route, the maximum difference in latitude is 15 degrees and the increase in distance is 700 miles – a quarter more. But the shortest route between San Francisco and Tokyo is 4,536 miles. By taking the Trade Winds route and going south to Hawaii, the maximum difference in latitude between the two routes is 20 degrees and the increase in distance is 1,060 miles, a little less than a quarter.

Thirdly, the start and finish of the Transpacific race were much farther south than for the Transatlantic. San Francisco is nearly on 38 degrees north and Tokyo 35 degrees, whereas Plymouth is on 50 degrees and Newport almost 42 degrees. Tokyo is roughly on the same latitude as Tangiers, and San Francisco as Lisbon. So the distance run to pick up the Trade Winds would be less than in the Transatlantic race.

The Great Circle or Orthodromic route meant sailing on a north-west course from San Francisco into an area where north-westerlies blow forty per cent of the time. This was as good as saying that it would be almost impossible to follow this route and that I should necessarily have to keep more to the south. The tactics would be to sail north-west during the sixty per cent of the time when the wind was not blowing from that direction, and to make westing when they did. That would not increase the distance by very much, and in any case would make fewer miles than by tacking in an obstinate attempt to follow the Great Circle route more closely. During the first leg of about five hundred miles the boat would be close hauled seventy per cent of the time, the winds on average would be Force 4, and there would be a strong likelihood of gales four per cent of the time.

Then, for the next 2,600 miles or so, westerly winds varying from south-west to north-west would be met, which would necessitate tacking. Their westerly direction would prevail the more I continued north-west, and become predominant as I went on a westerly course. The winds on average would be Force 5, and gales were likely about nine per cent of the time.

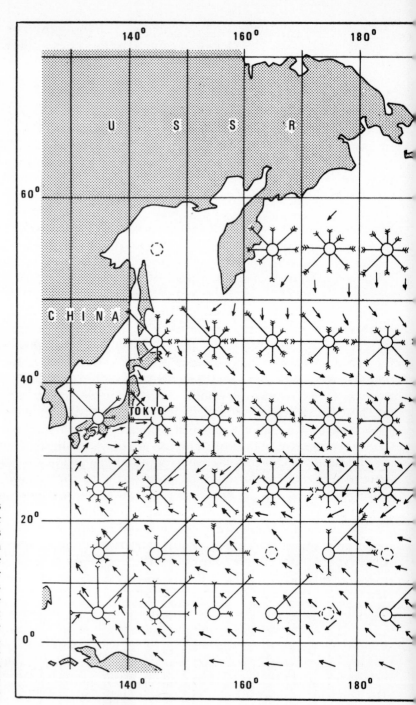

34–35 Pilot charts for the North Pacific showing probable winds and currents for March and April, based on the pilot charts for the previous year. The arrows indicate currents, the lines the direction that winds blow from; the length of line indicates the percentage, and the barbs on the end the wind force in terms of the Beaufort scale

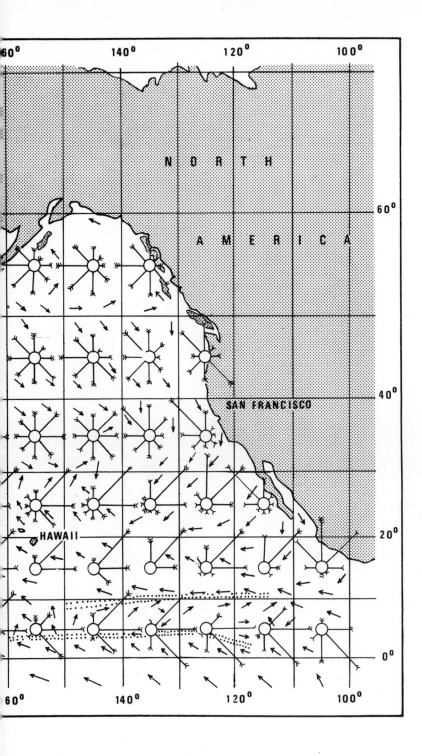

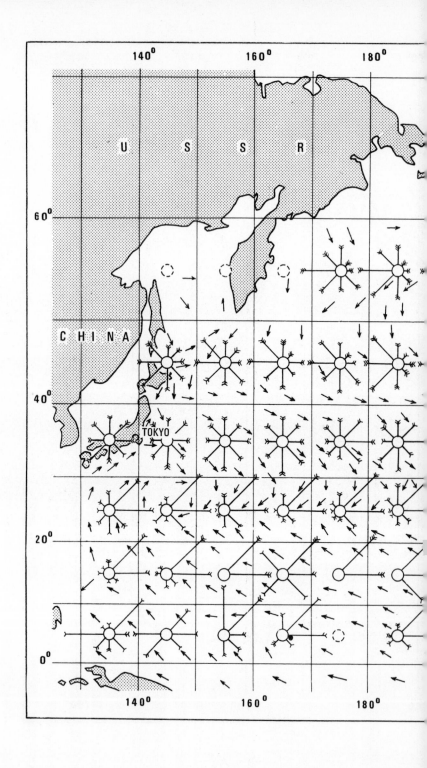

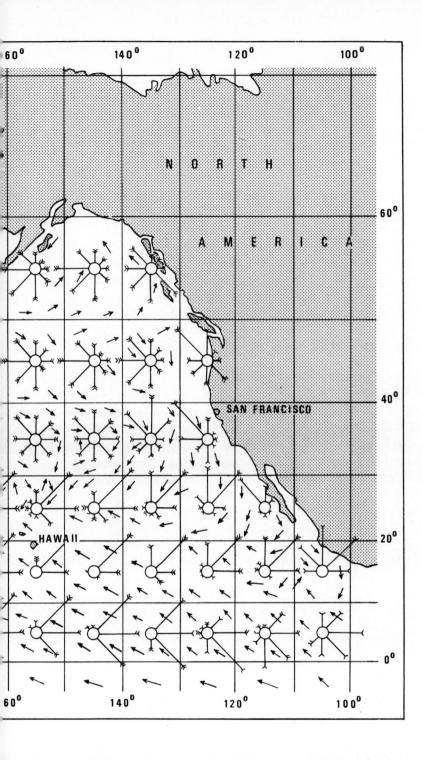

For the remaining 1,500 miles I should be heading south-west; north-west winds would predominate, with west winds twenty per cent of the time and south-westerlies twelve per cent.

By reckoning on covering the first 500 miles in five days, the next 2,600 in twenty-eight and the final 1,500 in twelve and a half days, and making allowance for the adverse current of about half a knot, this route would take fifty days.

The Trade Winds route meant sailing on a south-west course at first to pick up the Trades – about nine hundred miles with prevailing north-westerlies, Force 4, and west winds Force 3 for fifteen per cent of the time; with a slight risk of south-west winds Force 3 seven per cent of the time. Once I had picked up the Trades I would be on a westerly course, passing between Midway and Hawaii with the north-east trades well abaft the beam. And I would be in the Trade Winds, Force 4 on average, for about 3,600 miles. The final 1,200 miles would be covered in variable winds as I turned north-west towards Tokyo.

By reckoning on covering the first 900 miles in seven days, the 3,600 in the Trade Winds in twenty-five days and the final 1,200 in ten, and allowing for a favourable current of about a quarter knot, this route would take forty days.

Theoretically, then, the Trade Winds route was ten days the shorter.

The choice of this route explains why I asked for Pen Duick V to be a speedy boat in following winds. About 3,600 miles were likely to be sailed with the wind on the quarter. There would still be a good proportion of the route to be sailed in variable winds, when the boat would be close hauled for some of the time. The length of time I should be in those regions, about seven days and then ten days, were not long enough for statistics to be relied upon, and there was a likelihood of meeting headwinds for much of the way. Which was why the boat had also to perform well when close hauled.

6
A fast
lightweight hull

While Michel Bigoin and Daniel Duvergie were doing the paper work,
the La Perrière boatbuilders were already looking over samples and
ordering the necessary sheet metal and sections, in order to avoid
delays later through non-delivery. These orders were sent out although
there was still no real certainty that the boat would be built. I had not
yet found anyone to finance me. The previous spring I had put all I
owned into building Pen Duick IV, and I did not want to sell Pen
Duick III as I was thinking of entering her in more races later. Pen
Duick IV's broken masts had not been replaced and there was no hope
of selling her in her present condition. It was essential for me to find a
backer as quickly as possible.

I had been in touch with the yachting club at St Raphaël, and it now
offered to advance the money I needed. The arrangement was, in brief,
that the club would pay for the new boat, which would be registered by
and belong to the club; and I would repay the loan as and when I
could, and the boat would then belong to me. I was not thinking of
keeping the boat – I had enough already – but was hoping to sell her
after the race, in Japan possibly, so that I should be left owing the club
very little. In any case, I was now in a position to go ahead and give a
firm order for the boat, which was what mattered to me right then.

My two architects had their own particular way of working as
partners. One was in Marseilles and the other in Paris; each designed a
boat according to requirements, then they compared the two designs
and decided on one or the other, or made a new design based on the
best points of the two.

In my case, they submitted both designs (36, 37) to me first. Michel
Bigoin shows them to me when I went to Marseilles. I was rather
surprised to see that they were very similar, despite being the work of
two designers hundreds of miles apart. But they were used to col-
laborating and so had gradually adopted the same basic theories of
hull design. However, there was one major difference in the two
designs Michel Bigoin showed me. His (37) own had an innovation

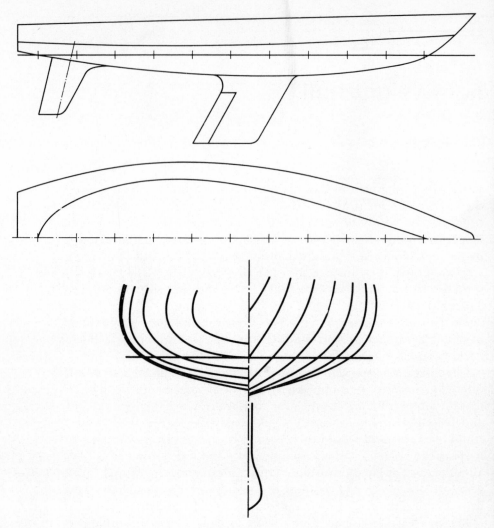

36 First version of Pen
Duick V. D Duvergie's
design 15.9.68

never before tried on a sailing boat – a knuckle going all round the hull above the waterline. The aim of this was to increase her stability when at more than a slight angle of heel. Bigoin had designed a few motor boats and had found that a knuckle increased their stability considerably when stationary. He could not guarantee that it would not be detrimental to the speed of a sailing boat, and the decision was left to me whether or not to make the experiment.

If there had been time to make a few tests in an experimental tank, the decision would have been easier. However, I liked the idea. Together we came to the conclusion that if the knuckle were well designed there was little likelihood of it acting as a brake. When

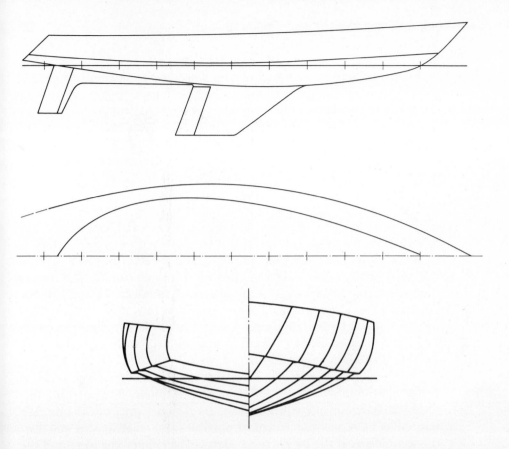

Pen Duick V. M Bigoin's
design 16.9.68

heeling over slightly her waterline beam was less than with a normal
hull with the same beam. When speeding along this knuckle ought to
have a dynamic effect which would increase stability even more. With a
following wind it should noticeably reduce the rhythmic rolling of
the boat; this was quite an important factor considering that the boat
would frequently be running before the wind. So, being naturally fond
of new ideas and fresh solutions when they appear sensible, I decided
to make the experiment. I was much influenced by wanting the boat to
be as light as possible so that she would plane over the water all the
better. Having cut down weight wherever possible and to the maximum, the only remaining way of reducing weight would be to have less
ballast, but then the boat's stability would decrease. Therefore, the
ballast could only be pared down and stability not be affected if an
increase in stability were obtained by some other means – and the
knuckle was one.

   I had gone to Marseilles with something else in mind. I wanted to put seawater tanks at each side of the hull. This would make it possible to pump the weather tank full in order to improve stability if need be. Such ballast tanks are not allowed under the rules of ocean racing, but they did not apply for this race, so we decided to fit them. With this stabilising element, the ballast in the keel could be cut down even further. We retained a little for safety reasons, calculating the minimum that would prevent the boat capsizing with the ballast tanks empty or with one or the other full.

There were no restrictions on the boat's draft either. I had this increased so as to get the weight of the ballast keel lower, where it does more good; this also enabled me to reduce the weight yet again, while still retaining her self-righting ability. Her draft was increased from 6 feet 6 inches to 7 feet 6 inches, and the ballast was reduced from 2,640 to 990 pounds. With the tanks holding 110 gallons the stability is surprising: the boat is kept as plumb when heeled at fifteen to twenty degrees as with a ballast keel of three tons and a normal draft. It was impossible to give Pen Duick V three tons of ballast in the keel, for her displacement would be only 3·2 tons when the tanks were empty. This lightness should greatly increase her ability to plane before the wind, and when close hauled in a good breeze, with the weather ballast tank full, her displacement would still only be 3·7 tons.

All this gave Michel Bigoin more work to do. As the ballast keel was being considerably reduced, the weight estimate differed and this meant a change in the volume of the underwater area of the hull. We wanted as light a displacement as possible, and what we did was this: the technicians at the La Perrière boatyard calculated the weight of the hull alone, based on the preliminary design and the samples of sheet metal, then calculated the weight of the rigging, spars, gear and accommodation, etc. and sent the total figure to the architects; they added the ballast considered necessary and designed the hull (38) in relation to the required displacement. As this had been reduced by 1,650 pounds with the ballast tanks empty and by 550 pounds with them full, we were able to reduce the hull's displacement by about 1,100 pounds.

But this was not all; the draft was also different and so the keel had to be redesigned. In order not to increase the underwater area, which should always be reduced to a minimum, the size of the keel was maintained; but the new one would be deeper and narrower, which would also give more grip and reduce sliding to leeward. With this in mind, we considered making the keel even narrower and so reduce the size even more. But we came up against a problem of resistance which was further complicated by a problem of hydrodynamics. For the keel

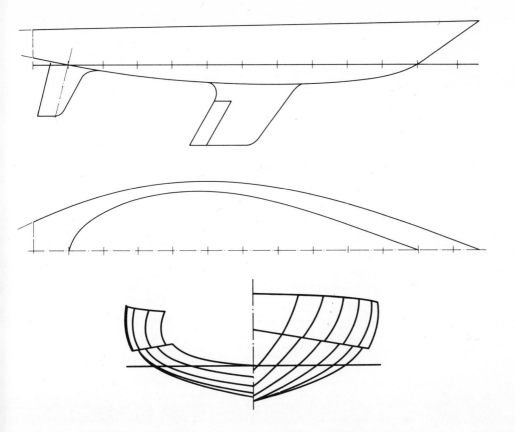

had to be strong enough not only to hold the ballast, but also to support the three tons of the boat if she went aground. So if the width of the keel were reduced then the thickness would have to be increased in order to maintain sufficient strength. There were obviously limitations if we were going to keep to a good length/thickness ratio and preserve the hydrodynamic qualities.

Michel Bigoin got down to work and soon had the final version of the design (39) ready for the boatyard, where the construction plan was at once drawn up. Despite all the modifications, we were still more or less up to schedule. We would work on the sail plan later, also the rigging, the accommodation and topsides. For the moment a rough plan was made in order to determine the centre of the sail area, which itself determined where the keel would be sited. If the plan had to be modified, a little resourcefulness would ensure that the centre of the sail area did not have to be changed in the fore and aft direction.

The final version gave the hull the following measurements: length overall, 35 feet; length waterline, 29 feet 6 inches. As the only rule for

38   Third version of Pen Duick V. Based on previous two and Tabarly's modifications 29.9.68

68

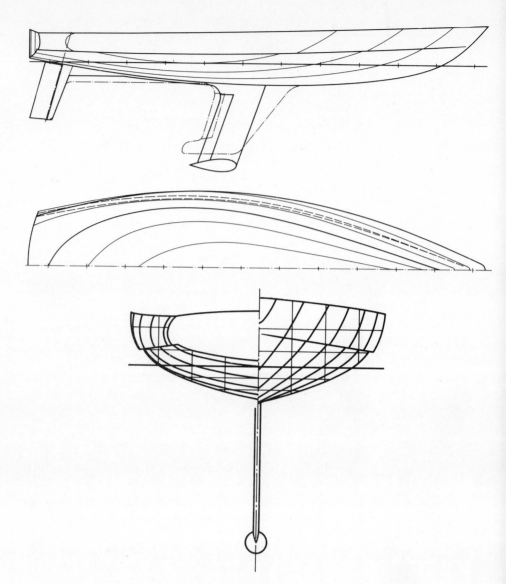

39 Final version of Pen
Duick V 2.10.68. Dotted
line shows the original
design of the keel;
thick line shows the
final form of keel and
trim tab

this race concerned the length of the boat, it might have been
worthwhile to build a boat with no, or almost no, rake to the hull, in
order to have the maximum useful length and therefore a possibility of
greater speed. As it was, there was hardly any rake at all to the stern;
and anyway, as soon as the boat acquired some speed she would be
pushed into the water up to her transom. This was slightly upswept so
that it would not drag in the water. However, Michel Bigoin and
Daniel Duvergie had given a rake to the stem, thus designing a hull

with nice clean lines; so what was lost in speed was more than compensated by her looks.

The boat's overall beam was 11 feet 2 inches, and the waterline beam was 8 feet 11 inches. The former was quite considerable and would give her good stability when heeling and also enable the ballast tanks to be situated as far as possible from the centreline, and so be more effective. On the other hand, the waterline beam was too narrow for the boat to push deep into the water. The difference between the two beams was not a result of the knuckle round the hull; the same effect could be obtained with a normal curved design. The advantage of the knuckle lay in having a shorter waterline beam when the boat was heeling slightly and in increasing stability.

The boat's displacement varied from 3·2 to 3·7 tons, according to the amount of water in the ballast tanks. Even with them full, this was a remarkably light displacement, due in part to the tanks themselves. For so efficient is this water ballast that the total amount of ballast (water tanks and keel) can be reduced yet still obtain greater stability than with just a normal ballast keel. Moreover, when the weight of the water is detrimental to speed it can be emptied back into the sea, thus lightening the boat for sailing in a gentle breeze and off the wind. However, the light displacement was chiefly due to the use of aluminium in her construction.

Ever since Pen Duick II I had been endeavouring to build light boats, although not always for the same reason. In the case of Pen Duick II and Pen Duick III I had wanted a boat which was both large yet easily handled for singlehanded racing. To that end, Pen Duick II had been built of plywood; but when I came to build Pen Duick III I had opted for aluminium alloy, which enabled the weight to be reduced even more. For the same weight of hull, the first boat had a length overall of 44 feet and 11 feet beam, while the corresponding dimensions of the other boat were 57 feet and 13 feet 8 inches. The gain, as can be seen, was considerable.

As for Pen Duick IV, she had to be light because a multihull cannot be speedy otherwise. By building her of aluminium alloy, this 65 foot trimaran had a displacement of just under 6·5 tons.

The reasons for Pen Duick V being built as light as possible were to increase her ability to plane over the water and her speed when sailing before the wind. The aim in this case was not a boat that could be easily handled by the lone sailor, as was essential with Pen Duick II, for the maximum length imposed by the rule of the race meant that the sail area would present no problem whether the boat were heavy or light. But for planing over the water every pound mattered. Due to the use of

Duralinox and to the very detailed work that the La Perrière drawing office put into the construction plan, the bare hull weighed no more than 2,200 pounds. This was achieved only by nibbling away wherever possible. If a bulkhead could be perforated, it was done; if the thickness of some of the metal sheeting seemed to have been over estimated, it was thinned down; wherever fittings could be combined with the structure of the hull, that too was of help.

While on the subject of aluminium alloy, I should like to mention its other advantages. In my opinion, it ought to be the material of the future for building yachts.

It makes a very strong as well as a light boat. A trimaran like Pen Duick IV is proof of this, for the various parts of this type of boat have considerable strain put upon them, especially the struts. As everthing can be welded, there is no longer any fear of even a drop of water seeping in. It puts an end to deficient caulking and leaking joints. But the great advantage is the little – almost non-existent – upkeep required with this light alloy. Painting is done only for the sake of appearance; and antifouling paint avoids the need for frequent slipping and scrubbing – and this paint will last a long time if the undercoats are carefully applied. I was surprised at how well it lasted on Pen Duick III. If you don't feel like putting any paint on at all, then skip it. This happened with Pen Duick IV and with the topsides of Pen Duick V. As the metal is rust-proof, there is nothing to worry about. After eighteen months afloat without a spot of paint on her, there is no sign of rust on Pen Duick IV. A boat built of light alloy can therefore be left afloat for several years and still be ready for sailing. There is no fear of marine life attacking the hull. If built of light alloy it remains as good as new.

The only danger is the possibility of electrolysis causing corrosion. But this is very slight, especially if care is taken never to bring another metal into contact with the alloy. The advantages of aluminium alloy are so great that Americans use it more and more, and even when not seeking to build a light boat. The weight saved on the hull is put to use elsewhere – either to increase the ballast, which is an interesting point, or to add to the equipment, accommodation and appointments. And so there are yachts – whose owners have no need to worry about cost – equipped with deep freezers, washing machines, salt water extractors, and so on, not to mention the little electrical installation to make it all work. So there is a very real gain, and for my part I would not build a boat of anything but light alloy.

The boat was on the drawing board by October, and the work of building her was able to begin. But there were still several questions to be settled on paper.

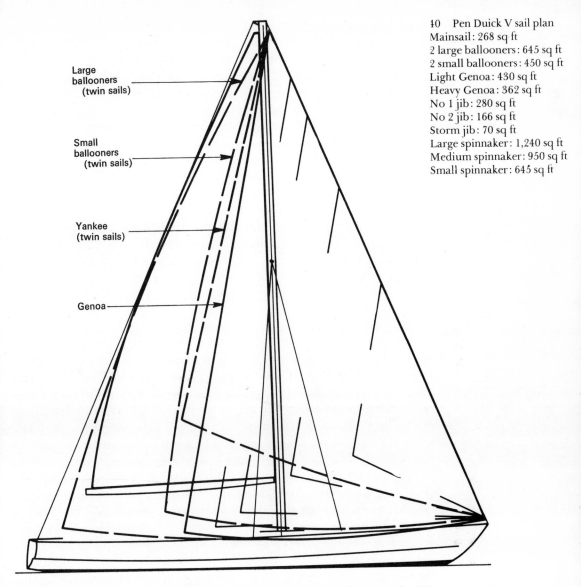

Large
ballooners
(twin sails)

Small
ballooners
(twin sails)

Yankee
(twin sails)

Genoa

40   Pen Duick V sail plan
Mainsail: 268 sq ft
2 large ballooners: 645 sq ft
2 small ballooners: 450 sq ft
Light Genoa: 430 sq ft
Heavy Genoa: 362 sq ft
No 1 jib: 280 sq ft
No 2 jib: 166 sq ft
Storm jib: 70 sq ft
Large spinnaker: 1,240 sq ft
Medium spinnaker: 950 sq ft
Small spinnaker: 645 sq ft

I went to Paris to discuss the sail plan (40) with Daniel Duvergie. He
thought the plan already sketched out gave a large enough area of
canvas, but for various reasons I wanted it to be larger.

First, the boat's great stability – much greater than that of other
boats of the same displacement – ought to allow a larger sail area.
Second, as I should have following winds for most of the race, it would
be a good thing to have plenty of canvas, for boats can carry plenty
when off the wind. And finally, the boat being small and the sails

therefore relatively small, there should be no difficulty about handling them, even singlehanded. Over canvassing the boat meant that there would be much changing of sails, because I should have to start shortening down sooner. However, taking for granted that ocean racing is a sporting contest and not a pleasure cruise, I did not think there was any need to be scared of that.

So I had the mast made taller. It would now be 40 feet 8 inches from the deck. This would allow me to set a mainsail of 268 square feet and a genoa of 408 square feet, which gives a very large sail area for a boat of 3·75 tons. Judging by normal standards, it was distinctly over-canvassing her.

She would obviously be given a sloop rig. I am in favour of dividing up the sail area for singlehanded sailing in big boats, and just as much in favour of a sloop rig for small boats, as the amount of canvas can be used to better effect. The value of a ketch or schooner rig is in the ease of handling the sails and not having any one large area of canvas. But obviously the efficiency of these rigs is not as good as that of a cutter or sloop rig. I felt certain I should have no difficulty in handling a mainsail of 268 square feet and a genoa of 408.

In order to carry plenty of canvas when running before the wind I needed large sails set on long booms. And to be able to stow them conveniently on deck I was going to have telescopic booms; when closed up they would be just under fifteen feet long – about the normal length of spinnaker booms for these boats – and would extend to twenty-five feet, with adjustment to three intermediate lengths. The sails were going to be spinnakers of various sizes and two pairs of ballooner headsails, a large and a small, arranged for roller furling. The largest spinnaker would be 1,290 square feet – quite a lot for the size of the boat. With the wind on the quarter or right aft I should rig it on the two booms extended to their greatest length and not carry a mainsail when the wind was directly astern. With the wind abeam, the lee boom would have to be taken in. It is very unusual to see a spinnaker set on two booms; as this is not allowed under ocean racing rules, many yachtsmen do not think of it. Yet we often did this when cruising in Pen Duick III; and everything was then wonderfully peaceful. With the spi billowing and held spread by its booms, there was no longer any weather roll. To gybe, all that was needed was to adjust the booms by easing away the one and hauling in on the other; the only other thing to do was to haul in on the mainsheet. With a following wind we thus sailed among the Swedish islands where, because of a shift of wind or the bends in the fairway, we were gybing every five minutes or so. But we had little to do other than adjusting

41 Pen Duick V
Length overall: 35 ft
Length waterline: 29 ft 6 in
Beam: 11 ft 4 in
Beam waterline: 9 ft 4 in
Draft: 7 ft 6 in
Ballast keel: 900 lbs
Displacement (with ballast tanks empty): 3·2 tons
Displacement (with weather tanks full): 3·7 tons
Cabin headroom: 5 ft
Headroom below deck: 4 ft
Architects: Michel Bigoin and Daniel Duvergie
Builder: La Perrière, Lorie

the mainsail, which was kept hoisted purely as a safety measure; if we had to take in the spi, because of a sudden wind shift, we quickly hoisted a jib and the boat was still easy to control – which was very necessary in the narrow waters of that archipelago. Moreover, with the wind on the quarter, the spi is well spread by its lee boom and is most efficient.

So with these advantages in mind, and as the usual ocean racing rules did not apply for this Transpacific race, I intended to rig my spinnakers from two booms whenever the opportunity arose.

The area of the two other spinnakers would be 970 and 645 square feet. I thought of setting those when I had a good wind abeam, and my twin ballooner headsails when the wind was abaft the beam or when running before the wind.

Each sail of the two pairs of ballooners would be respectively of 645 and 450 square feet, made of nylon with the larger pair of lighter weight than the smaller, and rigged for furling, or roller reefing for two reasons: because I had to be able easily to reduce sail according to the wind force, and because it is difficult in blowing weather for one person to haul down and get in a large headsail that is not set on the stay. But with a roller furling gear – I intended using a Merriman – the sail would be hoisted and taken in furled, rolled round itself. It would

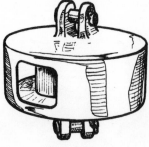

42 Swivel   43 Drum

be quite easy to lower, as the wind could not get at it. Otherwise, if I did not use this method, there would have to be two headstays for setting the two sails. But with two stays it is difficult to keep taut the one taking the strain when close hauled. The sail's hanks would get caught in the other stay, and anyway it is all unnecessary and misplaced weight.

The Merriman roller reefing gear works like this: at the head of the sail is a strong swivel (42) which must be able to turn easily even when there is a great strain on the halyard. At the tack is a drum (43) which turns with the luff of the sail and takes a wire rope, which is controlled from the cockpit. The sail is hoisted rolled up and by hauling on the sheet to set the sail, the wire rope is rolled round the drum. To reduce sail, or to roll it up before taking it in, all that is needed is to haul on the wire rope. This revolves the drum (44) which turns the luff and rolls up the sail.

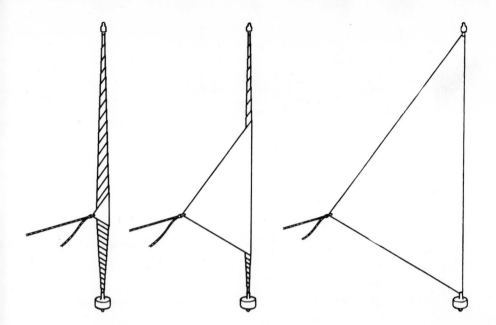

Having arranged all this with Daniel Duvergie, I went back to the La   44   Roller furling
Perrière boatyard to discuss the running rigging, accommodation,
pipes and cocks for the ballast tanks, the mast and the trim tab.

The accommodation was going to be as simple as possible, without
taking into consideration that at a later date there might be a crew
aboard, so as not to add unnecessary weight at this stage.

It proved impossible to have a similar companionway (45) and
cockpit as with previous Pen Duicks. Those boats had a companionway
from the well of the cockpit which was decked over by an extension of
the cabin top. The reasons for this were twofold: one was to provide
some shelter which could be used in turn by the crew on watch in bad
weather though this of course did not apply in the case of Pen Duick V,
not for the singlehanded race anyway; but the other reason was still
valid – to have an opening giving ventilation below all the time,
whatever the weather, without a drop of water coming in. Unfortunately this could not be done without giving Pen Duick V much more
freeboard. The well of the cockpit obviously had to be above the
waterline, for draining; but this was not possible – Pen Duick V being
very low in the water – unless the coachroof was built excessively high,
with all the disadvantages which would result from that. So I should
have to make do with the usual hatch (46) and put up with the
inconveniences. I should have to close the hatch in bad weather, and

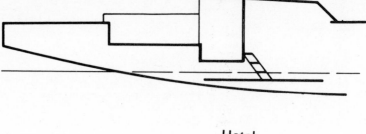

45 Companionway of
Pen Duick III

45 Companionway of
Pen Duick III

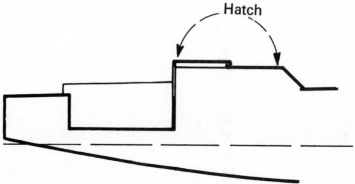

Hatch

46 Method of entry
for Pen Duick V

in order to have some air I should have to give up the idea of sealing
the after part of the coachroof with planks, and this meant that a little
rain and spray could always get in there.

When sailing in fine weather with the hatch cover off, one tends not
to close it soon enough if there's a sudden squall, and then the spray
gets in. To keep these inconveniences to the minimum I intended to
do as with Pen Duick II – to have a small compartment below the
hatchway, and in this would be the pump for the ballast tanks and the
sail bags. It was the best place to stow the latter anyway, for I should
have them close at hand when getting them on deck. This compartment would also be used to take off my dripping oilskins and so save
the cabin from getting wet.

Just forward of this compartment would be the galley and the chart
table, the former on the starboard side. It would contain only a
pressure cooker, a small sink with sea water and fresh water pumps,
and some plastic buckets fitting into holes in shelves. I had found this
arrangement very useful on Pen Duick III. All the utensils in constant
use can be dumped in the buckets and are easily taken out and cleaned
whenever needed. As on Pen Duick II and Pen Duick III I was going
to have a motor-cycle saddle on a pedestal fitted in the galley and
which could be adjusted to any height or angle. I should thus be able
to sit and cook a meal comfortably however the boat was heeling. I am

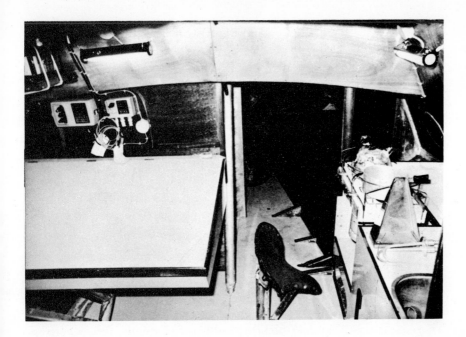

surprised that a similar arrangement is not found on other boats. I first
used it on Pen Duick II and I cannot do without it now. Cooking a
meal in rough weather is an ardous enough task not to make it as
comfortable as possible.

The same desire for comfort was applied to the chart table, which I
again intended to have as on my earlier boats – a table and seat
combined and which could be adjusted to the horizontal position
according to the heeling of the boat. So Pen Duick V was going to be
given a large chart table (47) worthy of a class I boat. It would take up
a lot of space, but there was plenty of that and from the point of view
of comfort was well worth it. This is a factor that should not be
disregarded, especially for a long crossing. All the energy saved by a
sensible and thoughtful installation in the galley and at the chart table
is that much more available for the handling of the boat, which is
obviously putting it to better use.

Further forward, below the mast, would be a compartment with two
bunks, one on either side. Some people may think this one too many for a
solo sailor. But both were very necessary for me to carry out my intention
of sleeping always on the weather side. On a boat of Pen Duick V's weight,
a man moving from the lee bunk to the other vastly improves her stability.
Above each bunk a compass would be fitted face downwards, so that I
could check the boat's course without having to get up.

47   The accommodation

The space forward of this compartment would be free for my supplies. In the space aft of the cockpit, which could be reached from where the sail bags were stowed or down the after hatch, I should put the spare gear, the light sails for setting in heavy weather, and the fruit.

Neither space, fore nor aft, was given bottom boards; and the accommodation merely had wooden battens to isolate contact with the metal hull. On the other hand, a coating of polyurethane foam was given to the cabin top and to the deck from below, with a covering of thin plywood, and I hoped this would help to keep out the tropical heat. Pen Duick III had been sprayed with polyurethane foam everywhere below decks, and as result this metal boat proved to be quieter than a boat built of wood. Pen Duick V was likely to be a little noisy, but I had saved a few pounds in weight, which was what mattered most.

The headroom, which for many is the test of good accommodation, was decidedly low. There had been little enough in Pen Duick II; but this boat, being smaller and flatter, had even less, despite the deck camber being rounded as much as possible to give a few more inches. There was only four feet of headroom in the small cabin where the bunks were, but this was of no consequence as I should go there only to sleep. The cabin with the chart table and galley had five feet of headroom, and there I should be sitting down.

Ventilation is very important, and I had quite neglected this on Pen Duick II. Fortunately that race had been in somewhat chilly regions, but after reaching Newport and a warmer climate I had found it impossible to remain below deck. I had deck vents fitted later, and in 1966 was able to live on board at Newport and in Bermuda. I profited from this experience when building Pen Duick III, which had all-weather ventilators and Goiot hatches that could be opened in fine weather and when in harbour, so that the boat was well ventilated. Now Pen Duick V was being fitted with three ventilating cowls, two Goiot hatches and two ports to the cabin.

There was no problem about the running rigging. With this simple sloop rig I had nothing like the trouble that Pen Duick III had given me. Pen Duick V had only a jibsheet, a mainsheet, and the spinnaker guys and sheets. A Goiot track along each gunwale from about five feet forward of the shrouds to the stern carried all the tackle, and there was a horse across the stern for the mainsheet to travel. Two winches either side of the cockpit took the jib and spinnaker sheets, and there was a small winch on the cabin top for the mainsheet. The lifts and down-hauls of the spinnaker booms and the roller furling for the ballooners were all belayed to cleats on either side of the cockpit. I should thus have all the tackle to hand and be able to handle the boat from the cockpit.

We discussed the shape to be given to the pulpit, with a view to belaying outboard of this not only the twin headsails, but also the jibs. The system introduced by Dick Carter is now banned by ocean racing rules. Yet it has many advantages. The jibs work better and are prevented from chafing against the wire stays or the pulpit.

The mast and standing rigging were ordered from a Swiss firm, Espars Nirvana, which was shortly supplying me with new masts for Pen Duick IV. The aluminium alloy of which their masts are made is so strong that weight can be saved without loss of strength. The sections as delivered are reinforced inside longitudinally at the place where the mast takes the greatest strain; this enables the thickness of the metal to be reduced, and so there is a further reduction in weight. It was important to reduce the weight of mast and rigging as much as possible because it had its centre of gravity eighteen feet above the deck, which meant a leverage that was detrimental to the boat's stability. There would be only one pair of crosstrees, which is the best rig for a masthead sloop, where there is no need to brace the jib stay. Two sets of crosstrees would give a less sensible rig and a heavier one. Instead of lower shrouds forward there would be an inner forestay. This would save more weight and would also prevent the jibsheets from getting snarled up, when tacking, with the cleats and winches at the foot of the mast. The shrouds were coming from the makers which had supplied me with them since Pen Duick II was built. Before delivery the wire is stretched to the utmost, so that when the rigging is set up it is as taut as it should be, and there is no need to adjust it later because of stretch.

All the halyards would be concealed inside the hollow mast, to avoid wind resistance. As well as the mainsail and spinnaker halyards there would be two for each of the twin ballooners. This is best and safest for a long crossing as the headsail halyard gets a lot of use and may sometimes wear through and break. All the halyards would lead down to Goiot winches. I greatly favour this system which leaves the base of the mast clear, and I've never had any trouble with Goiot winches. The only precaution is to see that the wire winds evenly round the barrel to begin with, so that the rest follows on correctly; there will then be no trouble provided the tilt of the winch is properly adjusted. Otherwise the wire is liable to wind round anyhow, and then it soon gets damaged and needs replacing.

The pipes and cocks for the ballast tanks set a few problems. There were going to be two pairs of tanks, and I had to be able to drain or fill

80

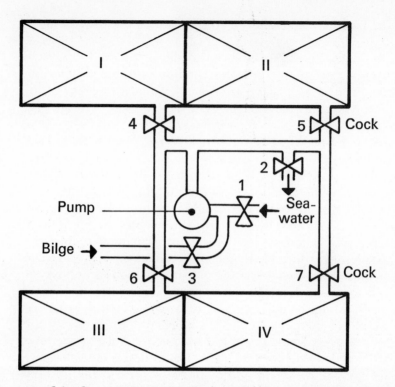

4 ▷◁ 5 ▷◁ Cock

2 ▷◁
1
Pump ──── ⊙ ▷◁ ← Sea-
water

Bilge → ═══
▷◁

6 ▷◁ 3 7 ▷◁ Cock

III IV

any of the four; and it had to be possible for the water in the windward
pair to pass into the other by gravity due to the heeling of the boat. To
facilitate this, we decided to have the widest pipe that could be fitted to
the plastic cocks. Seven cocks and several feet of piping would do the
job (48) and even enable the bilge to be pumped out. For instance,
supposing tanks I and II are the windward tanks and I want to fill
them. I open cocks 1, 4 and 5 (all the others being closed) and pump
up the water, then close those cocks. If I then want to pump water from
the bilge, I open cocks 3 and 2. Afterwards I close them again.
Supposing I want to go on the other tack and to shift the water
to ballast tanks III and IV – before changing tack I open cocks 4, 5, 6
and 7 and the water is drawn across by gravity; I then close the cocks
and go on the other tack. If I then want to drain away some of the
water in tank III I open cocks 2 and 6, then close them when enough
water has been emptied into the sea. And if I want to empty the lot, I
open cocks 6, 7 and 2. So I could have whatever amount of water I
wanted for ballast just where I wanted it. The system may seem
complicated but in fact it was quite simple to work, as the cocks were in
the obvious places. In any case, a mistake would not be disastrous.
Water could not get into the bilge if cocks 2 and 3 were left open, as the

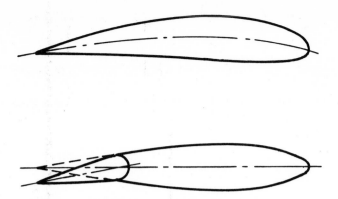

pump blocked the flow; nor could it get into the bilge if cock 3 were
open when a tank was being emptied into the sea. The only danger was
if cock 3 were left open by mistake while filling one of the tanks. Then
the water pumped up would flow into the bilge instead of the tank, and
quite a few gallons might well get in before the mistake was discovered.

There had to be an air outlet to the tanks, and so two pipes led up to
the cabin roof, one on either side and which were also used as hand
grips. The water level in each tank could be checked by means of a
transparent plastic pipe.

There remained only the question of the trim tab – the adjustable
flap fitted to the after edge of the keel. The object of the trim tab was
not to help steer the boat (that being the sole function of the rudder,
placed well aft) but to increase the lift of the keel. By deflecting the tab
a few degrees, the centreline of the keel is given a curve, and a curved
shape (49) in hydrodynamics, as in aerodynamics, has a better lift than
a straight one. Aircraft have trim tabs – elevators – at the trailing edges
of their wings to increase lift when flying at low speeds. In any case, the
trim tab's function was to reduce leeway. As is well known, the keel and
the underwater area of the boat must develop sufficient resistance to
balance the force of the wind on the sails. This force heels the boat and
tends to make her sheer to leeward.

The sea strikes the keel at the angle at which the boat is sheering to
leeward. The lift given by the waves depends on the shape of the keel
and the angle and speed of the waves. For a given wind strength and a
given speed of the boat, the lift will be equal and opposed to the force
of the wind on the sails at a given angle of leeway; for example, six
degrees. If the shape of the keel is improved and conditions remain
unchanged, the same lift is obtained with an angle of leeway of, for
example, four degrees. This is what the trim tab does. Thus the boat
when close hauled would beat to windward two degrees better. There is

a slight influence on the speed, as the hull drags more through the water.

Another effect of the trim tab as an addition to the keel is that it slightly moves aft the centre of lateral resistance of the keel; and this helps to offset the tendency of some boats to become uncontrollable when a following wind freshens. However, I was not counting much on this in Pen Duick V's case; her keel was very narrow, so the effect would be exceedingly slight.

On Pen Duick III the trim tab was controlled from the cockpit by a crank that turned a worm screw; the screw operated a slide which acted upon the wires leading to the trim tab. The spindle of the trim tab was carried into the boat through a stuffing box. I wanted a simpler arrangement for Pen Duick V. The trim tab had to be controlled from the cockpit, of course. Pierre Fouquin solved the problem – the spindle could be carried up to the deck, which meant just forward of the cabin, and the wires would lead in tubes each side of the cabin roof to a small rod below the tiller, and which could be locked in various positions according to the desired angle of the trim tab. The wires would be kept taut by a couple of rigging screws. This was much simpler, and ought to work satisfactorily.

7

The solo
sailor's auxiliary

A well adjusted and perfected self-steering gear is a piece of auxiliary equipment that is practically indispensable for a singlehanded long distance race. A solo sailor cannot remain at the helm for twenty-four hours for days on end, so the boat must steer herself while he is working or sleeping.

There are a number of very simple and rudimentary self-steering gears in use, and some solo sailors who are little concerned about preciseness of steering seem quite happy with them. But there are other self-steering gears, more elaborate and very ingenious, which act very well indeed and have been perfected in recent years, due chiefly to the experience gained in singlehanded races.

In my previous book Lonely Victory I described the simpler systems and their general principles: if the boat alters course, the relative wind direction changes and it strikes the vane on one of its faces; this pressure corrects the rudder, and the boat comes back on course. This system has two great disadvantages – lack of power and inadequate synchronization of the vane.

A wind vane pivoting on a vertical axis (50) can only do so at an

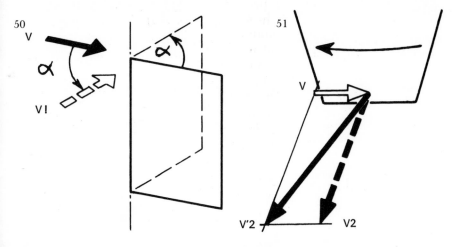

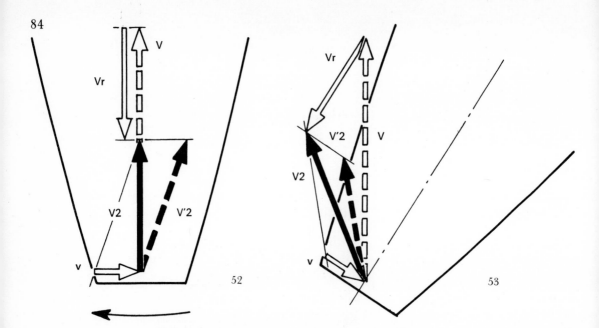

52

53

angle corresponding to that of a change of wind. But when the wind is light and there is only a slight shift of wind, the vane does not exert sufficient force to correct the rudder. It loses power in the transmission and it pivots at an angle even slighter than the shift of wind. The vane only exerts sufficient pressure on the rudder to bring the boat back on course if the alteration has been considerable. This disadvantage is particularly noticeable in light following winds, when a good deal of helm has to be applied to counteract the tendency to yaw.

If the boat yaws, the wind movement set up the swing of the stern affects the vane (51). This wind V nullifies the effect of the actual wind direction V2, or rather shifts it to the direction V'2. Consequently the angle of the vane does not synchronize with the change in direction of V2 in relation to the fore and aft direction of the boat, as it should do, but shifts with the change in direction from V2 to V'2, and leaves the vane at V'2 in relation to the fore and aft direction of the boat as she edges off course.

However, this can be an advantage when sailing to windward, for the yawing of the boat has an opposite effect. Supposing the boat is sailing to wind (51). The boat's change of course brings V2 in relation to the fore and aft direction of the boat round to V'2. So the vane will be at the correct angle for countering the yawing of the boat, and at a wider angle than if there were no V. In other words, the yawing is an aid to the vane's action. This advantage is minimal,

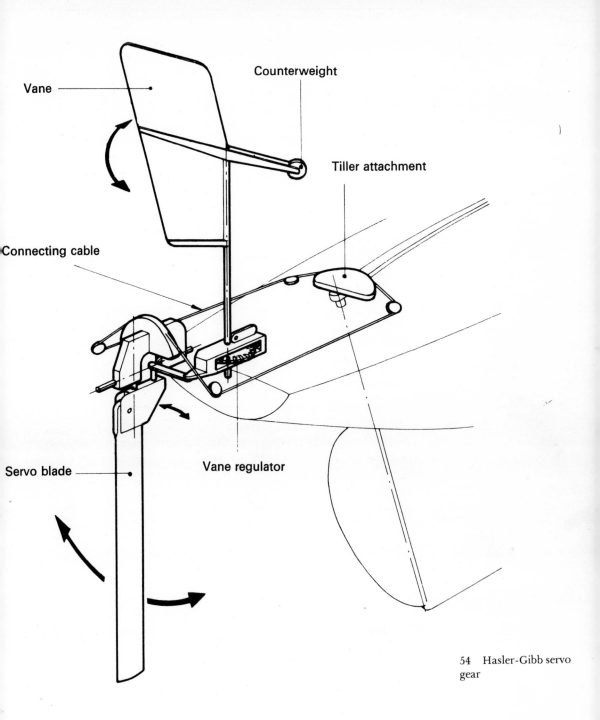

Vane

Counterweight

Tiller attachment

Connecting cable

Servo blade

Vane regulator

54   Hasler-Gibb servo gear

however, as a boat going to windward is well balanced and any yawing is slow and slight.

But when sailing with the wind astern the disadvantage of this inadequate synchronization is considerable (52, 53). When the boat yaws, the vane shifts through the action of V'2 – in the opposite direction to that needed to counter the yawing, which will be accentuated until the change in the boat's course alters V2 enough to bring it into line with V'2. The initial direction of V2 is (53) that of the actual wind V. But the above would equally apply with the wind on the quarter.

The conclusion to be drawn is that when sailing off the wind these simpler self-steering gears induce an erratic course that reduces the speed of a boat.

Several self-steering gears have been invented to try and overcome these disadvantages, and two at least have given good results.

In 1964 Colonel 'Blondie' Hasler tried to overcome the problem of the vane's lack of power by having the vane act upon a long servo blade (54) instead of directly upon the tiller. The small surface area of the servo blade meant that it could be easily shifted by the wind vane. Its leverage is considerable, acting upon an axis parallel to the longitudinal axis of the boat, and it is attached to the tiller by a line running through pulleys. This gear has the required strength but does not overcome the problem involved when sailing before the wind.

The disadvantages were overcome by the system invented by Monsieur Gianoli and developed by the Eca firm. The innovation here, introduced by Gianoli in 1962, was to have a vane, or aileron, pivoting on an oblique axis.

The relationship of the angles in 55 is shown by the following formula, where c is the pivot of the vane, b the slant and a the wind change.

$$\frac{c = a}{\sin b}$$

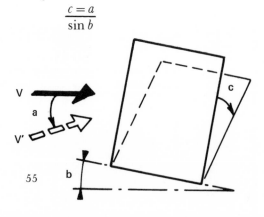

55

sin b being less than 1, and c greater than a.

Then, for instance, where a equals 1 degree and b equals 10 degrees, c will equal 5·6 degrees; and where b equals 1 degree, c equals 57 degrees.

The model (56) I used for the 1964 Transatlantic race had the slant b at 10 degrees and so the work of the vane was 5·6 times greater than one of the usual kind and of the same size, and acted upon a small balanced rudder. To improve synchronization when sailing before the wind, a turbine was mounted behind the vane so that when the boat yawed, the movement effected the turbine, whose action trimmed a flap attached to the forward edge of the vane and the flap caused the vane to pivot correctly for countering the yawing of the boat.

I did not find this entirely satisfactory, as the flap often had a delayed action. In a heavy swell, V (the wind movement set up by the swing of the stern) became very great in relation to V2, which was then not strong enough to turn the turbine.

Monsieur Gianoli took note of this, and when I asked him to supply me with another model for my singlehanded Atlantic crossing in Pen Duick II in 1966, he produced his improved self-steering gear MNOP 66.

The vane pivoting on an oblique axis was retained, but the b angle was 7 degrees instead of 10, which when a equalled 1 degree gave c 8·2 degrees, thus increasing the power of the vane. The turbine was abandoned, and a servo blade took over its role. It was an adaptation of an aircraft aileron invented by Gianoli before the war and which he called an autoptère.

The aim of this improved version (57) was to correct the action due to the swinging of the stern. When the boat yawed, the direction of the jets of water striking the blade would change according to the speed of the deviation, and this would put to good use by deflecting the blade so that it countered the yawing.

The autoptère blade or rudder (58a) consisted of an over-compensated plane, P – that it to say, the pressure it exerted was applied from a point forward of its axis of rotation, O – and of an articulated flap at the tip of P which automatically shifted when P shifted.

Supposing P is shifted when in a steady current, V, then f × l prevails over F×L, and P returns to a direction parallel to the current.

But supposing (58b) current V is deviated to V', the lift F shifts P, producing a shift of the flap in relation to P, and the blade returns to a balanced position when F × L is equal to f× l. Thus, whenever a yawing movement sets up V', it would be at once countered by the deflection of the blade, and by a force applied at O equal to that resulting from F

88

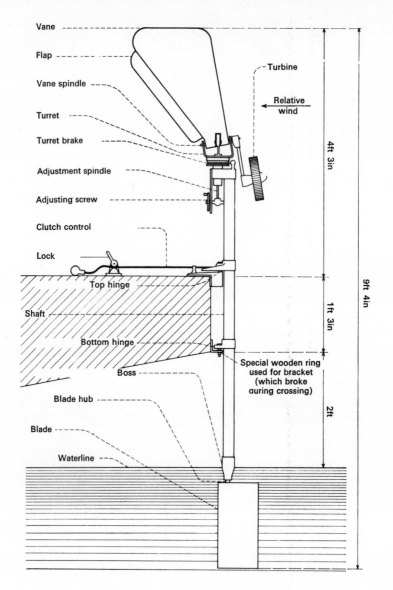

Vane

Flap

Vane spindle

Turret

Turret brake

Adjustment spindle

Adjusting screw

Clutch control

Lock

Top hinge

Shaft

Bottom hinge

Boss

Blade hub

Blade

Waterline

Turbine

Relative
wind

4ft 3in

1ft 3in

2ft

9ft 4in

Special wooden ring
used for bracket
(which broke
during crossing)

56 MNOP 64   and f. Because of the curved shape of the blade, this force O was much greater than it would have been with a straight blade – an important additional advantage.

Yawing being thus countered by the action of the servo blade, the vane's role was that of a direction indicator to keep the boat at a steady angle in relation to the wind, which it did by shifting the flap which in turn adjusted the blade.

This self-steering gear worked very well during my Atlantic crossing

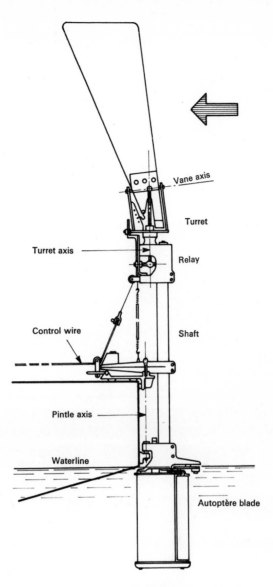

Vane axis

Turret

Turret axis

Relay

Control wire

Shaft

Pintle axis

Waterline

Autoptère blade

57   MNOP 66

in 1966. Its one defect was due to the fact that it had been designed for use on small boats and was not always powerful enough to steer a boat of Pen Duick II's size. When, with a following wind increasing in strength, the boat became lively, the servo blade shifted in the required direction all right, but did not exert sufficient force to bring the boat back on course; and then I had either to take the tiller or take in some canvas.

Nevertheless, this MNOP 66 had been greatly strengthened in com-

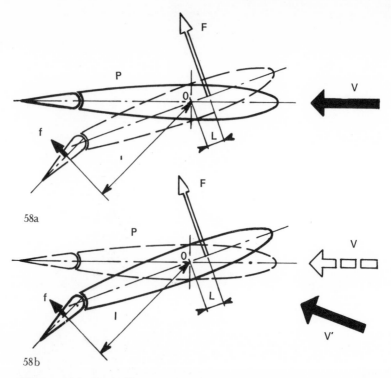

58a

58b

parison with the self-steering gear which had let me down during the 1964 race, when a spindle broke in the shaft. In his calculations, Gianoli now allows for four times as much force being put on the servo blade. This makes the gear heavier but sturdier.

A model of this kind was used on my trimaran, Pen Duick IV. It was quite complicated, because the boat's rudder had been conceived for use in conjunction with this self-steering gear, but when the latter was disengaged it had to be possible to steer with the tiller. Gianoli ingeniously modified the gear (59) so that there was a smooth change over from steering with the tiller to steering with the vane, and vice versa. However, there had not been time before the race to test it sufficiently, any more than some of the other equipment and rig, such

Memo from M. Gianoli: With the MNOP self-steering gear, the boat's sails have to be trimmed, course set and the rudder locked before the gear is engaged. On Pen Duick IV the autoptère rudder did duty for the boat's rudder, and it was thought that the parallel hulls of the trimaran would give the same stability as the locked rudder of other boats equipped with a MNOP gear. But this was not so, and the autoptère rudder pivoted with the swerving of the stern. We tried increasing the control exerted by the shutter, but this remedy was not sufficient so the response of the autoptère was reduced by decreasing its over-compensation from 35 to 30 per cent. This took a day to do, and since then this self-steering gear has functioned efficiently in all weathers.

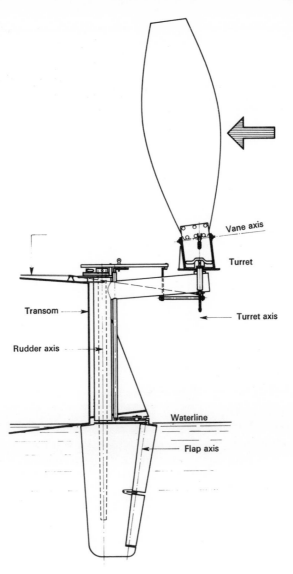

Vane axis

Turret

Transom

Turret axis

Rudder axis

Waterline

Flap axis

59   Self-steering gear
for Pen Duick IV

as the rotating masts. This experimental model was the cause (there would probably have been others, apart from that) of my retiring from the Transatlantic race soon after the start. It worked too well! When speeding along, the boat was kept on course to within a degree, but the apparatus vibrated so badly that it shook itself to pieces.

I now had to decide on the self-steering gear for Pen Duick V. It would take too long, I thought, to have the one used on Pen Duick IV repaired and converted for use on a smaller boat, not to mention the cost. And besides, there was a serious disadvantage to that model – if it broke down I might be deprived not only of a self-steering gear but be unable to steer the boat at all. I preferred to have a self-steering gear that worked independently of the boat's rudder.

Pen Duick V, which was smaller than Pen Duick II, ought to be all right equipped with a MNOP 66, which had been much improved and had given every satisfaction to the four competitors – Foezon, Paillard, Piazzini and Terlain – who used it in the last Transatlantic race. Foezon and Terlain sailed the Atlantic both ways without any fault occurring in the self-steering gear, which was proof of its sturdiness. I intended taking a spare with me, just in case.

8

Pen Duick V
comes to life

The hull was almost finished by November. It was being built upside down, as both Pen Duick III and Pen Duick IV had been. First the deck was placed upside down on steel stocks (60) then the ribs were added, the inboard part of the keel and the strakes (62) and finally the sides (63). The hull was then reversed, and the keel (65) and ballast (66), the rudder and deck fittings were added. The reason for this manner of building the boat was to facilitate the work of the welders.

I missed by a few days seeing the hull turned the right way up, as I had to set sail in Pen Duick IV on November 26.

I needed to be in San Francisco before the start of the race on March 15, but Pen Duick V would not be ready in time to be sailed there, and would have to be shipped. Besides, her first trials could not possibly be held before the end of December. So I intended to make use of this interval by sailing Pen Duick IV across the Atlantic, which I had been prevented from doing in June. I wanted to try out the boat properly, and at the same time I might find a buyer for her in the United states. I knew that Pen Duick IV was a speedy boat, but I wanted to prove that over a long distance she was a good sea-going boat, reliable and faster than a monohull. Moreover, this would confirm whether she was really the right boat for the singlehanded Transatlantic race and whether the troubles I had with her (excluding the brush with a cargo vessel) were simply due to her lack of preparation. In addition, I thought that after the San Francisco to Tokyo race I might try to break the Los Angeles to Honolulu record when that race took place; although the race itself is for monohulls, the record for the crossing is open to multihulls as well, and was then held by Ticonderoga, a 72 foot monohull.

So, while seeing the boatyard people about the various matters already explained, I was also busy with Pen Duick IV. She had not been sailed since the rotating masts broke in July. In August I had taken part in the Yarmouth to Santander and the Santander to La Trinité races with Pen Duick III, quickly given a ketch rig, and at the

60

61

62

60–63 Pen Duick V on
the stocks: the hull was
constructed on the
upturned deck, then the
whole was reversed.
(Pen Duicks III and IV
were built the same way.)
64 A milling machine
at work on the keel
65 The hull without
ballast or rudder
66 The ballast for
Pen Duick V's keel

63

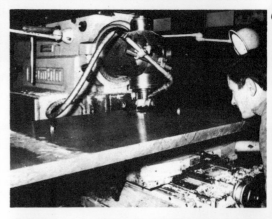

66

end of September I began seeing about new masts for Pen Duick IV. I decided against having her rotating masts repaired, and to use the insurance money on buying new, standard masts. I'd had enough disappointments with those rotating masts. Not that I disapproved of the principle; it is a good aerodynamic solution, and I feel sure it can be put into effect. But in Pen Duick IV's case the masts were handicapped by the inadequate shrouds. The experiment needed to be begun all over again, but unfortunately I did not have the necessary funds; yet I was still greatly interested in the idea. However, I ordered standard masts from the Swiss firm of Espars Nirvana, the only firm able to deliver in the short time available. They arrived at the same time as the new shrouds. The boatyard welded new chain-plates to the hulls, and by mid November Pen Duick IV was ready to sail again.

The self-steering gear had always been troublesome and several efforts to improve it had been made. We had tried increasing the control exerted by the flap, but this made little difference. Before setting sail to cross the Atlantic I made another attempt – not that I really needed the self-steering gear, as I had two crew, Olivier de Kersauson and Alain Colas. But I thought it a pity for such an ingenious mechanism not to work properly, and felt that all it needed was some quite simple modification. It worked well when the boat was sailing slowly, and if Pen Duick IV had been a monohull there would have been no problem. But we ought to be able to get it to work well at speed. There was one part we had not touched – the over-compensated autoptère rudder. I had this over-compensation reduced, and the response greatly improved. The fierceness with which the gear corrected the boat's course – the cause of it breaking down – was diminished. On the other hand, its response when sailing slowly was not so good as before, though this did not prevent it from working properly. But it was asking the impossible to expect it to work perfectly all the time, at speeds which varied from one to twenty knots.

Everything was then ready, we took food supplies on board and at twelve thirty on the afternoon of November 26 we sailed from La Trinité for Fort-de-France, Martinique. We arrived there on December 19, having put in at Teneriffe and then making a record Atlantic crossing in ten and a half days, which was an average of eleven knots.

I flew back to France from Martinique to be in time for the final work on Pen Duick V and to try her out before shipping her to San Francisco. The Compagnie Générale Transatlantique had very kindly offered Jean-Yves Terlain and me free transport for our boats, and they were to be loaded on the Maryland at Le Havre on February 2.

I reached Paris on December 23, and on Christmas Day saw Pen

Duick V in the boatyard at Lorient. She was not finished, but there was not a lot left to do. The boat looked just as I expected, with her wide, flat hull, compact lines and generally aggressive air and speedy looks. I was glad to see her like that. A few days' work on her were still needed to complete the deck fittings and accommodation, put in the ballast and instal the piping for the tanks. I was right to be there while this final work on her was being carried out. This was the time to decide on many small details and adjustments that cannot be foreseen on paper, and there is no one better to decide than the person who is going to sail the boat. Only when standing in the cockpit can one say, 'I want this winch just here and this cleat there.'

I drove up to Paris on December 30 to get the electronic equipment, the speedometer and the wind indicator, and other fittings from the General Marine shop. Before starting back to Lorient, to set my mind at rest I phoned the boatyard to ask about the mast, which was due to be delivered in a day or two. I was told that the mast was ready, but I had to arrange transport for it from Espars Nirvana in Switzerland. Another unexpected difficulty: the masts for Pen Duick IV had been delivered to the boatyard by a haulage contractor who had a special trailer to hitch on to his truck, but he was not available and I had to find some other means. This was a blow. The boat was going to be launched on January 4; if I had no mast, there would be a delay in taking her out for trials. The New Year holiday was about to begin and even if I could find a means of transport it would very likely cost the earth. If I could lay hands on a suitable trailer I would go and fetch the mast myself. The General Marine shop knew of no one who could help. I phoned Pierre Fouquin, who was in Paris, but he could not think of anyone either. As a last resort my brother suggested using the trailer on which he moved his own boat. It was rather light for the purpose, but was better than nothing. It was at my parents' house near Angers. I had no tow-bar on my car, but I could take advantage of going home to borrow my father's car, which did have one. Pierre Fouquin kindly offered to go with me to Switzerland so we could take it in turns to drive.

I set off at once for Angers. On the way I stopped at the Marco Polo factory, near Chartres, and picked up the telescopic booms, tying them on the roof of the car.

Leaving my own car with my parents, I started back to Paris in the early evening with my father's car and the trailer. I got Pierre Fouquin out of bed in the middle of the night and we drove to Switzerland, reaching Yverdon and the Espars Nirvana firm by midday on the 31st. We had a quick lunch, then got the mast loaded on to the trailer. It had to rest on its side and it projected over the car almost as far as the front bumper. However, it seemed secure enough and we set off. We could have chosen a better day – there had been snow on the roads nearly all the way from Paris, and it was the same going back. But with the mast in tow, driving was even more difficult and we had to take great care. Because of its length, the mast developed a considerable up and down swaying motion, assisted by the springs on the trailer, which were very supple. This motion was conveyed to the car, and when this became too pronounced the only thing to do was to keep the wheel absolutely still and wait for the swaying to die down.

We greeted the New Year on the southern motorway and were at Pierre's by three in the morning. He gave me a bed, and after breakfast I left at nine to continue the journey alone. As soon as I got on to the western motorway I realised that things were very different from the previous day. With only one person, the car was too light, and when the mast began swaying it carried the car with it and I had to slow down. I couldn't do more than forty miles an hour. There had been a heavy fall of snow in the Orne, and traffic had left deep ruts; the trailer began swerving dangerously, the mast accentuated the movement, and suddenly I found myself facing the way I had come, with the offside wheels in the ditch. But the car was all right and so was the mast, which was the main thing. The only damage was to the trailer, which had lost a wheel. Fortunately, on this New Year's Day a garage happened to be open in the next village. The mechanic went back with me and collected the wheel and screws, did the repair job at the garage, and back we went again to replace the wheel. I set off once more. There had been a partial thaw early in the afternoon and the roads were better. I got to Lorient late at night, very glad that the expedition was over. What boats lead you into, though!

On January 3, with Victor Tonnerre the sailmaker, we rigged the boat with her halyards and shrouds, and next day she was put afloat and the mast was stepped.

The first time I sailed the boat I was much impressed by her. Yet when at the helm and close hauled, I did not seem to be sailing very fast. The speedometer had not been fitted, but when Pierre Fouquin came out in his Zodiac to take some photos and I went aboard for a moment to have a look at Pen Duick V I could tell that in fact she was making great speed and sailing powerfully. I thought that my impression when aboard her was due to the fact that she sailed so very smoothly – not much splashing at the bows, little foam and a very flat wake (68). There was a Force 4 wind and the boat was sailing with the smaller, but heavier genoa up and the windward ballast tanks full.

67   Launching
Pen Duick V

68   Pen Duick V planing
– note the smooth wake

Pumping the water up had been all right, except that it took twelve to thirteen minutes of continuous work to fill one pair of tanks completely. A few days before, Alain Gliksman had told me about a rotary pump, a Vortex, that ought to work better. I could couple it up with the existing Anderson pump, though it would have to be adapted slightly as the Vortex isn't intended for this kind of work; and besides it isn't watertight. I must just accept the possibility of having a slight leak there. Otherwise, it all worked well. The ballast could be shifted from one side to the other very quickly, in about two minutes. With the lee side tanks full, the boat was heeled over at about forty degrees (69), but this was not dangerous as even then she still answered the helm easily. Emptying the water back into the sea was very quickly done too.

I took the boat out to sea about every other day during this period, for the boatyard was still finishing off some minor jobs and there were the necessary alterations that became evident from the boat's trials.

On the very first day it became apparent that the pipe to draw water up into the ballast tanks was sited too far from the centreline of the boat. When on the starboard tack and heeled at an angle of 20 degrees, this pipe was out of the water and so it was impossible to pump. It had to be sited as close as possible to the keel. Then two safety foot grips had to be welded forward of the mast, because the high camber of the deck made hoisting a sail a tricky business when on the lee side. Also the halyard winches needed adjusting to a better angle. Each time, we found something that required attention. For instance, the telescopic booms did not lock properly – the flat spring holding the locking screws in place was made of some inferior metal and would not hold.

69 Just before tacking the water in the weather ballast tanks has been transferred to the lee tanks. The boat is well heeled and the mainsheet has been eased, but Pen Duick V nevertheless responds well to the helm

70 Pen Duick V close
    hauled off Lorient
71 A sudden gust lays
    Pen Duick V over
72 Pen Duick V begins
    to plane

The screws were replaced by bent pins, not so practical, but more reliable, and there was no time to do anything better.

The speedometer was fitted and then I had a closer idea of the boat's speed, which reached seven knots when sailing to windward (70), if the speedometer's reading was correct, and seven and half knots on occasion, with a Force 4 wind. For a boat of Pen Duick V's size, this was remarkably good. We took her from one tack to another, making an angle of 90 degrees – not quite so good as the best craft, but a very honourable performance.

When sailing before the wind she was very fast indeed. With a Force 4 wind and the small spinnaker of 645 square feet set (72) we were making ten knots – which was what I expected of her.

Two things about her performance which were a pleasant surprise, for I had not reckoned on them, were: first, that despite her wide beam the boat could heel quite a lot without losing speed; at 25 degrees the speedometer showed no drop in speed, only when the heel approached 30 degrees. Second, again despite her wide beam and wide stern (73), the boat was steady to the helm however much she heeled. Her smooth and quiet manner was most pleasant. During the whole of these trials

when, it must be admitted, there was never a really big swell (74) the boat showed no inclination to shoot into the wind.

73 Sailing to windward

To test her speed I should have liked to sail her against Pen Duick III, which I had kept afloat at La Trinité expressly for this purpose. Unfortunately, the school holidays were over and my crew who were students, Philippe Lavat and Pierre English, had to leave; my brother Patrick, Gérard Petitpas and Michel Vanek were away preparing for the Paris Boat Show; and Olivier de Kersauson was at Fort-de-France, looking after Pen Duick IV. So I had no one experienced enough to

74 Close hauled, in a
slight swell

sail Pen Duick III and there was no opportunity to compare the two boats. We met only one boat while out at sea, an Arpège. Close hauled in a gentle breeze, under the large genoa and without any water in the ballast tanks, we were much the better on course and in speed. I also noticed that my speedometer was not inclined to exaggerate, as judging by the speed of the other boat the six knots it gave us seemed more than likely.

Altogether I was not dissatisfied with these trials. However, there were two important items I was unable to try out: the self-steering gear and the twin ballooners. Of the two self-steering gears I was taking with me for the race, the new one was not yet ready, and the other, bought secondhand from Piazzini, was still being overhauled. As for the twin sails, Victor Tonnerre had not received the material in time to make them for the boat's trials. All of these were later stowed in the boat before she was shipped to San Francisco, but without my having been able to test them.

It's an amazing thing, but before each singlehanded race I never seem to have more than a very short time for trials, and even that goes awry. The first time this happened. before the 1964 Transatlantic race, I said to myself – never again, next time I'll start preparing earlier. begin building the boat in good time, so I shan't set off so ill-prepared. And each time, for various reasons, the boat has been launched at about the last possible moment.

With Pen Duick II it was lack of money that prevented me from starting building her earlier; the plans were ready a long time ahead, but we were held up. Pen Duick III was built well ahead of time and I should have had a year of sailing her before the start of the race. But then I became convinced that a trimaran would do better and got André Allègre to design Pen Duick IV. There again, the plan was ready in good time but several months went by before I could get the money to start building the boat. Consequently she had hardly any trials, when at least three months were needed to try out such a boat, which had some fittings and equipment – for instance, there were the rotating masts – that were experimental. And now here I was engaged again in a race against time, on this occasion because I had not known sooner that there was to be a Transpacific race. Fortunately, one knows better what one is doing with a monohull, and I hoped to avoid the unpleasant surprises I'd had over Pen Duick IV.

Part Three

San Francisco to Tokyo

9
Getting to
the start

I arrived in San Francisco by road on March 7. I had intended to arrive in Pen Duick IV, and so we had sailed from Panama on Feburary 2. I was expecting to make a very slow passage because of the calm weather and, later, the contrary winds we would meet with; but I thought that nevertheless it was not over optimistic to reckon on the trimaran covering the 3,500 miles in a month. We never made it, partly because of the adverse weather conditions, but chiefly due to something unexpected -- we lost the centreboard on the third day. We made hardly any progress when close hauled, and there was plenty of that. When I realised that we were not going to reach San Francisco in time, I made for San Diego, the first American port beyond the Mexican frontier.

We put in there on the night of March 5, then spent the whole day looking for somewhere to berth the boat for a few days. There were no moorings in the harbour but plenty of marinas; none of them, however, would have her because of her size. She could not remain any longer at the Customs quay, so we decided that Olivier and Alain should set sail again for San Francisco while I hired a car to finish the journey. That evening I transferred from the boat to the car everything I should need aboard Pen Duick V, and on the morning of the 7th I was in San Francisco.

I firmly believed that Pen Duick V had been there waiting for me for several days. But I discovered that the ship bringing her from France, the Maryland, had been held up in Los Angeles by a dock strike and was not expected to reach San Francisco until late on the 8th, a Saturday, which meant that Pen Duick V would not be unloaded until Monday morning the 10th. This was a blow, and I was worried at the thought of all the things still to be done, and at the strong possibility of having to forego taking Pen Duick V out to sea for trials a couple of times, as I had intended. By starting work that day, the 7th, there would have been only just time to do everything; as it was, there was going to be the usual rush and bustle once again. No doubt about it – I was never going to be well prepared at the start of a race! It was annoying not to have known of this hold up before changing course for San Diego, because then we might all have reached San Francisco in time for the unloading of Pen Duick V, and that would have eased things considerably for me.

One of my sailing friends and occasional crew, Jean-Michel Carpentier, had been waiting for me in San Francisco for the past few days. He was to look after Pen Duick IV while I was away, then go sailing with me. He had been given hospitality by Claude Reboul, an ex-officer of the French Naval Air Arm, who lived in San Francisco. Claude Reboul proved to be my saviour; he invited me to stay with him, and, thanks to his help, in five days almost everything there was to be done got done.

There was in fact a whole week before the start of the race, but little could be done for the moment. Still, I made a few purchases – some tools and crockery – and saw boat dealers about the possible sale of Pen Duick IV and V. As I was thinking of building another Pen Duick, the sixth of that name, it would be very useful if I could find American buyers for numbers IV and V after the race.

The Maryland duly docked on the Saturday evening, and Jean-Michel and I started work on Pen Duick V early Sunday morning. There was a repair job to be done on the after edge of the ballast keel, which had been damaged at the Boat Show; we made that right with glass fibre and resin. Then there were the electronic wind indicator and the alarm course indicator to be fitted up. The latter had been taken out of Pen Duick IV at San Diego for me to use now. It is a very useful apparatus for a solo sailor – it can be set so that he is wakened by the alarm whenever the boat goes twenty degrees off course, or thirty or forty. We also finished installing the pump to fill the ballast tanks, as there had not been time to do this in France. Finally we got the mast ready to be stepped on the Monday morning, as soon as the boat was put afloat. Altogether it was a very full day and I was glad to have been able to get so much done.

We were back aboard the Maryland early next morning. Jean-Michel and I each had a paint roller and we gave the boat a fresh coat of antifouling. The coat she had been given at Lorient before the launching was still whole, but it must have aged and lost some of its potency. A fresh coat was very necessary if I was not to be slowed down by a foul bottom before reaching Tokyo. By then the boat would have been afloat for nearly two months, much of the time in warm waters that encourage marine growth on a hull.

Much of my morning was lost, as was only to be expected, in customs

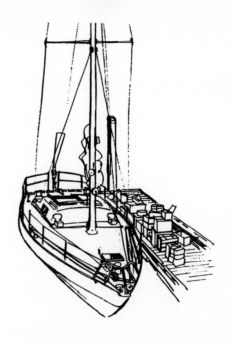

formalities and paperwork. However, just before midday a floating
crane lifted Pen Duick V into the water, also Jean-Yves Terlain's boat
Blue Arpège, another entry in the race.

In the afternoon Pen Duick V's mast, which was lying on her deck,
was stepped with the aid of a sling from the Maryland. Terlain adopted
a different method; his mast was still aboard the ship, and it was
lowered as his boat lay alongside. When both boats were ready we were
taken in tow by Claude Reboul, whose boat had a powerful motor. San
Francisco Bay is very large, and as the Maryland was berthed right at
the eastern end of the docks on the southern shore there was a long
way to go to reach the San Francisco Yacht Club on the other side of
the bay. There are at least ten clubs around the bay, and despite its
name the one we wanted is not at San Francisco, but at Bellevedere, on
the northern shore. A very good yacht club, well equipped and most
comfortable. Only one of the other competitors was there, an
American, Jerry Cartwright, who had arrived two days before. He had
a new boat, thirty-five feet long, the maximum allowed for the race
and which was said to have been specially designed for it. She seemed
to me, however, to be little out of the ordinary and neither her lines
nor topsides gave the same impression of effectiveness that Pen Duick
V did. Cartwright had a very large sail area due to a projecting boom.

76

77

78

76   Jean-Yves Terlain
77   Eric Tabarly
78   Claus Hehner
79   Jerry Cartwright
80   René Hauwaert

79

80

His self-steering gear looked rather like Hasler's, but had a vane of the Gianoli kind – that is, it pivoted on a roughly horizontal axis. Jerry Cartwright was a tall, hefty young Texan with a friendly air, and he had sailed down the coast from Oregon, where his boat had been built.

So there were three of us, two being French, and three more competitors were expected – a German, a Belgian and another American.

The German, Claus Hehner, arrived next day in his Mex, a Tina that he had shortened by a foot at the stern to bring her down to the regulation thirty-five feet. I thought he would be my most serious rival, for his Mex had already proved herself a very good boat, and I was glad that Pen Duick was going to be pitted against her. We should see how it turned out.

Two days later the Belgian, René Hauwaert, arrived from Los Angeles. His boat was a steel built, fore and aft rigged yawl that did not look at all like a racing boat. He had been sailing her singlehanded about the Pacific for a long time.

The sixth entry, the other American, did not turn up, having retired from a qualifying singlehanded cruise from Los Angeles to San Francisco. So in the end there were only five competitors, three of whom – Terlain, Hehner and myself – had made one or more singlehanded Atlantic crossings.

Right up to the start there was much for me and my helpers to do. Claude Reboul looked after electrical problems and also saw to my food supplies. I had stowed some non-perishable food on board before the boat left France, intending to obtain fresh food here, especially fruit – bananas, oranges, apples, lemons, pineapples together with vegetables, tomatoes and cucumber. Claude made sure I had plenty of all that, and I even had some Californian wine. Jean-Yves Terlain found that he had too much tinned food and gave me some, so that in the end I think I must have had enough food on board to last me to Tokyo and back again. I also bought a typical American food – ready-cooked pancakes. Americans eat these for any meal and with all sorts of food. I had only to add some water and then brown them in the pan; I should pour maple syrup over them, which is a popular way of eating them in the States. I also bought a supply of smoked salmon too – there was plenty on sale and it was very cheap, as salmon abound in these waters. Luckily it happens to be a favourite dish of mine, and I was looking forward to it. In short, for the moment I had the impression of setting off on some gastronomic cruise.

81 The two French boats (behind La Belle Poule, centre) with Mex (right) moored at the San Francisco Yacht Club

I had a small battery tape recorder and in the evenings I recorded some of Claude Reboul's large library of LPs, so that I should be able to listen to music now and again while crossing the Pacific.

Jean-Michel and I were busy trying to get everything in order in time aboard Pen Duick V, cleaning up and checking over the rigging and equipment. Fortunately Claude Reboul was able to lend me a car, otherwise I should have lost much more time whenever I needed something, for we were a long way out of town. For instance, there were two stainless steel bolts holding the self-steering gear to the stern, which had been made thicker at that point, and I wanted to change them as I was afraid that electrolytic action might eat away the threads of the screws and the bolts would come adrift. So I thought of isolating the steel from the Duralinox by inserting the bolts in hard plastic tubes, embedded in glue. This would remove all risk of electrolysis. But first I needed two other bolts. I had a whole boxful on board, but of course there's never the size you want. So I had to go into San Francisco to get them, and that took a whole morning. Thanks to Claude, however, time lost in one way was retrieved in another. He moored his boat La Belle Poule (81) alongside Pen Duick and I was able to have at hand his wide range of tools, which included an electric drill that was most useful. Moreover, we had our midday meal with him, which saved us going miles.

On the Wednesday afternoon before the race I took Pen Duick V out to sea. This was absolutely necessary in order to check the running rigging and to see how the boat behaved with the self-steering gear in command. I also wanted to try out the ballooner headsails' roller furling gear. As mentioned earlier, neither the headsails nor the self-steering gear had been ready in time for the boat's trials at Lorient.

Directly after lunch we hoisted sail, slipped our moorings and sheered off – or rather we tried to, for the boat would not budge an inch. It was low water and we were stuck in the mud. I then realised why I had seen only small boats at this clubhouse. Pen Duick V was a small boat all right, but with the draft of a large one – seven feet six inches – and those moorings were clearly not the best for us. Jean-Yves Terlain came in then and gave us a tow to just outside the harbour (our keel leaving a furrow in the mud), but then he ran out of fuel and turned back, leaving us stuck there to wait for the tide to come in. In order not to waste time I experimented with the large ballooners and their furling gear. The system worked all right, except that the wire going round the drum was too short. I should have to buy some more wire to make it long enough for the sail to be completely rolled up. Then a motor launch came and towed us out to deep water. It was five o'clock and the wind had dropped. The self-steering gear worked satisfactorily in these light airs, but what would it be like in a good breeze? It was too late to do more than hope for the best.

10
Seeking the Trade Winds

The morning of the 15th had arrived. I was up early as I had four important letters to write, including one to my parents. I had bought some envelopes, but of course they were on the boat. So I wrote my letters before leaving Claude's apartment, intending to put them in envelopes when I got on board and to mail them at an office I had noticed near the clubhouse. But what with the briefing by the race organizers and their final instructions, being interviewed by reporters and the preparations for the start, I completely forgot about my letters! At sea that evening, to my consternation the first things I saw on opening my bag were the precious letters. There was no question of turning back to mail them! They would have to wait until I got to Tokyo.

The start was at noon, so just before 10.30 Claude came to give Jean-Yves and me a tow across the bay, as the starting line was in front of the St Francis Yacht Club on the San Francisco side of the bay. There was very little wind indeed and we should have taken too much time getting across under sail. Jean-Michel was at the tiller and I continued my efforts to get some order into things, thinking it would still take a few days before a place was found for everything. On a long crossing such as this, many supplies had to be taken and stowed away; but the rudimentary accommodation on this small boat did not help attempts at tidiness.

Meanwhile a wind had got up from the west, a nice Force 4 breeze, and the sun was shining. It was indeed a fine day for a sail. At 11.45 I made sail, the tow was cast off and Jean-Michel went aboard Claude's boat. I was thinking it would be necessary to tack to get out of the bay, but the tacks would be too short to justify making use of the ballast tanks, as in going about to send the water from one side to the other I should lose time that could not be regained. So I hoisted the No 1 jib, keeping the genoa for when I was beyond the bay and on a long board with the weather ballast tanks full. With the No 1 jib I had all the canvas needed and the boat was nicely heeled at fifteen or twenty degrees.

There were sailing boats and craft of all descriptions out to see the start, a great crowd of them milling about. The starting gun went and I crossed the line, but it was a poor start. It would have been much better if I had not been afraid of crossing the line before the gun went, but there was a strong four knot current flowing out of the bay, and I thought I should lose a lot of time if I got carried across the line and then had to turn to re-cross it. The gun went just as I started to bear away, and I had to gybe to get her round again, for if I had luffed her up I should have missed passing the buoy marking the end of the line. However, the boat went round very quickly and I found myself just astern of Claus, who was himself astern of Jerry, who had made the best start. An interesting little race then ensued. I soon overhauled Claus's Mex, passing to windward, and then Jerry. There was no doubt that this boat of mine designed for running before the wind was nevertheless formidable when close hauled, for Mex's ability to go to windward was well known. Pen Duick would have sailed even faster with one ballast tank full and the genoa set. Jerry seemed to me to have some curl in his sails; his boat was heeled a lot, and yet he had a reduced mainsail.

We left the bay accompanied by the crowd of spectators' boats, and it was very necessary to keep a sharp lookout. Just ahead of me a nondescript boat with old sails and shabby rigging lost way while going on the other tack, and I had to luff almost into the eye of the wind. Other boats calmly took my wind without seemingly having the least idea that they were hindering me. For instance, a sailing boat larger than Pen Duick and using her motor passed a few yards to windward with her crew waving in friendly fashion. Before I had time to pick up speed again, an even bigger boat shaved past on my lee, causing me to lose a few more yards. Fortunately this was not the start of a regatta race and the few lengths I had lost would not affect the result.

Going under the Golden Gate bridge I already had a good lead; I tacked as I neared the northern shore, which took me back across the entrance to the bay on a south-west course, which was the right course for Hawaii. But I was no longer in the current running out of the bay and would soon be overhauled by the other competitors, who had remained in it. So I tacked again and, the wind having fallen away, hoisted the genoa. For the rest of the afternoon there was only a slight wind, which dropped completely at times, and in order to remain in this current – which mattered more and more as the wind fell away – I was obliged to sail a peculiar sort of course.

I could clearly make out the limit of this current, for it was marked by a winding line of eddies. So I had to wind about with it, which at times caused me to be on a broad reach when my course was to windward. Eventually the current curved to the north-west and ceased to be of any help at all, so I tacked to the south and left it. My tactics must have been good, for I was in the lead again. As night fell I could see only two boats astern of me – those of Jean-Yves and Claus. I was rather surprised to see the latter on the same tack as myself, for he had said before the start that he was going to take the Great Circle route. He must have changed his mind, or he would have been on the other tack.

I was beginning to have some difficulty with the self-steering gear in this rather variable wind. It functioned very well provided the tiller was correctly adjusted. Its rudder was just aft of the boat's rudder which, having a larger area, was much more powerful; so that when the wind strength varied, the tiller had to be re-adjusted. The self-steering gear ought to have had enough strength to bring the boat back on course instead of following the boat's rudder. But I had to keep a constant watch and adjust the tiller as the wind varied. This was something that Gianoli had feared, as he explained in a letter he had put in the chart table before the boat left France. He would have preferred his self-steering gear to be mounted on a framework instead of being fixed directly to the transom, as that would have brought it further aft and by increasing the leverage would have increased its efficiency. Moreover its rudder would then have been clear of the water disturbed by the boat's rudder – which must cause a further loss of efficiency.

Unfortunately I was not in France at the time, so he was unable to talk to me about it. He added in his letter that the reason for his not mounting the gear as indicated was because he feared infringing the rule limiting the boat's length overall to thirty-five feet. But the rule did not prevent him from doing that. When reckoning the length overall no notice is taken of adjuncts such as projecting booms and self-steering gears. It was a great pity that we had not been able to discuss the matter before I left France; and in view of the difficulties I could now see ahead I bitterly regretted that this modification had not been carried out when it had been possible to do so.

I very much doubted whether the self-steering gear would function any better in a strong wind. In any case I foresaw the worst with the wind abeam, even if blowing steadily. On that point of sailing a boat tends to be unstable; once she loses her delicate balance, she is unlikely to regain it; if she is brought closer to the wind she will continue to luff, as she will take charge of the steering, and if she falls off the opposite occurs. I was beginning to take a rather gloomy view of the future.

That first night at sea was spent continually adjusting the tiller. I set the course indicator and about every half hour its alarm went and I had to leave my bunk either because a light squall had caused the boat to luff or the squall had died down and she had fallen off.
From the log

March 16

Still close hauled, but the wind has steadied. The weather is fine and although the breeze is light the boat is making five or six knots. I take advantage of these good conditions to spend the day doing odd jobs. I prepare the lacings and reef pendants I need, and make the tackle for a boom downhaul. I also put up the aerial for my receiver – very necessary to have the correct time when taking a sextant sight of the sun. This is the only way I have of fixing my position and navigating across thousands of miles of ocean.

In the afternoon the sky clouds over, the wind hardens a little, and I decide to fill one pair of ballast tanks. It is the first time I have used the new Vortex pump, which proves to be a little quicker than the Anderson. Unfortunately it is very exhausting to work; to maintain a good flow you have to turn the handle very fast, and this is difficult to keep up for long. Still, I filled the tanks in eight minutes (as against twelve with the Anderson), but only by a strenuous effort that left me as breathless as if I'd just run an 880 yards race. I'm not sure I shall go on using this pump. In any case, as expected, it leaks and lets water into the bilge. In these boats with a flat bottom, having water in the bilge is the very devil. It only needs a few pints and when the boat is heeled the water rises all along the side and wets everything you've put there. You can't pump it out, as there isn't enough for the pump to get at; you have to go and bail it out with a tin and a bucket, and then mop up.

At 16.00 hours it starts to rain and the wind veers forward, becoming south-west. I go on the other tack to make westing, being on a southerly course. The wind continues to harden and at about 18.00 I change the genoa for the No 1 jib. There is now a Force 5 wind and the waves are getting bigger. Pen Duick is sailing very well, making seven knots or more. Pity we're not heading south-west, which is where I want to go. However, the percentage of south-west winds is small in this area, and I have hopes of the north-westerlies blowing up before long.

March 17

The wind falls during the night and at about 01·00 I hoist the genoa again. At 03.00 I let out the water in the ballast tanks. Am now making no more than three knots in a slightly choppy sea. The night is again very cold, and very damp as well. At daybreak there is a thick mist.

About midday, still a lot of mist and hardly any wind. I employ my time doing more odd jobs, giving priority to the rigging. I increase the length of the wires to the headsails' roller furling, adding as much as the drum can take. I'm still not sure that it will be enough, but it's impossible to add more. I shall see before long. I extend the wires with a short line so that I shall be able to haul on them from the cockpit when they're fully wound round the drum.

At about 17.00 the wind gets up a bit and veers west. I go on the other tack and so am at last on the right course, heading south-west or almost, but still close hauled and not sailing very fast.

Making four or five knots during the night. Temperature still low. The salad oil has frozen in the bottle and the butter is difficult to spread. Still, I am going towards the sun.

March 18

Still on a south-west course but wind still light. However, the sun is shining and I'm about to take my first sextant sight and at noon make my first fix.

Have progressed in the right direction, but only for 270 miles. In three days, that makes an average speed of just under four knots. What are those Force 4 north-west winds doing? I ought to be having them according to the pilot charts.

In the afternoon the wind drops again and there is almost a flat calm. A heavy swell from the north-west is coming abeam, making the boat roll and the sails flap. I don't like these sort of conditions – they're bad for the sails, the genoa in particular, which chafes against the shrouds and the end of the crosstrees every time the boat rolls, and is being subjected to more wear than the progress it makes is worth.

March 19

At about 01.00 the wind veered very quickly north-east. I now have the wind astern and it is freshening a little. I have set one of the larger ballooners on the starboard boom, taken in the genoa, and set the other big ballooner. Then I lower the mainsail so that it shouldn't take the wind out of the ballooner on the port boom.

08.00 hours. I have taken in the ballooner on the starboard boom as it has torn. I can't understand what has caused this. Certainly not the light breeze. It was the first time I'd used the ballooners' furling gear, and I find that the wire still isn't long enough. The canvas is so thin that to roll up the sail completely far more turns are needed than there's enough wire for. I don't

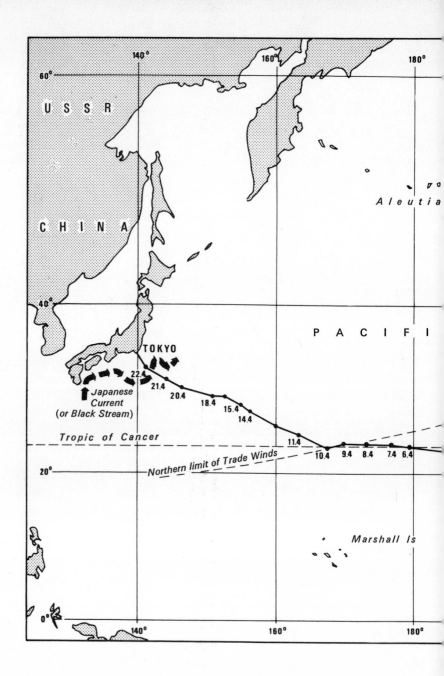

82   Tabarly's route in
the Transpacific Race

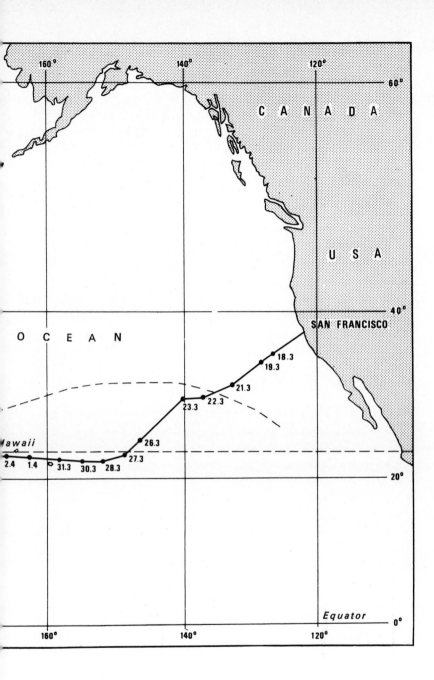

see any solution. I hoist one of the smaller ballooners in place of the torn sail. The weather is lovely.

At about 10.00 the wind shifts forward and I have to take in the port ballooner. I hoist the mainsail again and get in the starboard boom, then spread the big spinnaker. With the wind abeam, a light breeze, it draws the boat along nicely, thanks to its large area. This is the first time I've spread it and its size is impressive, seen from such a small boat.

11.30. The wind shifts further forward and I have to take in the spinnaker. I hoist the genoa.

The breeze freshens at about 13.30, and I pump up some ballast. Am now close hauled and making eight knots. For the first time since the start the boat is speeding along on the right course. But the barometer is falling and the weather is getting thick and looking unsettled – and to think what a fine morning it was! The wind is still shifting forward and I'm now hugging it. I certainly shan't be getting a north-westerly today. By 16.00 the wind strength is Force 5, and I change the genoa for the No 1 jib. Pen Duick is sailing well, pitching a little in a sea that's beginning to heap up, but she's maintaining speed. I've often noticed this with light boats in a good breeze; they pitch, but still make good speed. It happened with Pen Duick III, which now and again pitched quite heavily.

At 17.45 the steamer Tenbury, of London, makes a complete circle round me. Very seldom do you see a merchantship take so much interest in a sailing boat. Some of them slightly alter course to pass nearer, but the majority steam straight on.

The weather is now dull and grey, and a cold drizzle has set in. Moreover, with the wind still hauling round I am being edged more and more off course and am heading westward. By 20.30 the board I am on is taking me more degrees off course than if I were on the other tack, or in other words, for the same distance covered I should approach nearer to my destination on the other tack. So I go about. This is the first time I've gone about with the wind so strong, and it is very satisfying to find that the shifting of the water from one pair of ballast tanks to the other, before going about, is successful. The boat heels a lot but not overmuch, as I luffed while the ballast was being shifted and at a moment when the sails were just about to shiver. The wind continues shifting after I have gone on the other tack, so much so that I am heading south-west again. It's a pleasure to be back on the right course – you feel you haven't been wasting your time so much.

However, conditions are becoming more and more uncomfortable. At 22.00 I take a reef in the mainsail. The wind has increased to Force

6, and there are waves quite twelve feet high and plenty of foam. The boat is pitching more heavily but is still making about seven knots. At midnight this has dropped to six, and the boat is labouring. She is carrying too much canvas. The rail is under water all the time. I take another reef in the mainsail – this eases the boat and she is soon making seven knots again.

March 20

The shocks against the bows keep getting harder. I've never known a boat shudder like this before. Everything is vibrating, as though the whole rigging will come down at any moment. I'm not easily shaken as a rule, but I must admit I feel a bit uneasy.

At three in the morning I take in the jib, for the wind has suddenly increased and is now Force 8. The No 2 jib would probably hold, and certainly the storm jib, but with only the bit of mainsail up she is making five knots. It's not a lot, but the lurching has stopped and I prefer things like that for the moment. It must have had a slightly traumatic effect on me. I'll have to get used to it, for after all nothing ought to break.

The wind eases just before 11.00 and I run up the No 2 jib. She is sailing at a fair pace and in a more seemly manner now.

And so she continues for the rest of the day. Unfortunately I feel too shaken to tidy up or to stitch the torn ballooner.

March 21

Weather improving a little. At 06.00 I change the No 2 jib for the No 1. At 07.00 I let out the two reefs and, as the wind veers aft, I ease the mainsheet a little.

The fine weather has returned. At 10.30 I hoist the genoa. The sea has subsided, the sun is shining. I shall be able to take a noon sight. I begin repairing the ballooner.

At midday my position shows I have progressed 280 nautical miles in the right direction in the past 48 hours. This average of 5.8 knots while close hauled in bad weather, and not always on the right course, is fairly satisfactory; but it could have been better if I had not let myself be influenced by the mad way the boat was pitching. Another time I shan't continue as I did for hours, just under the reefed mainsail; that lost me more than one knot. She can lurch as much as she likes, she can take it.

At 18.00 the wind veers aft enough for me to set the big ballooner headsail on the starboard boom.

Five hours later – and I find it ripped across in the same place as the other was. There's a mystery here, that I must get to the bottom of, for at this rate I shan't have much chance in the race. I haven't finished

repairing the other sail yet, so now I'm without a single big ballooner.
I set one of the smaller ones.

March 22

This morning the wind is right aft, so best results will come from
rigging the big spinnaker on its two booms. By 08.30 this is done. The
weather is magnificent, it's really warm for the first time since the start.
The butter I had this morning was quite soft. I bring up a few bananas
to try and ripen them before the others, so as to spread out the meals
with bananas on the menu.

At midday, just a week out, I am 875 miles from San Francisco,
which gives a daily average of 125. It's not a lot, but considering the
calms and the contrary winds, it's not too bad. Still, I was reckoning on
having the north-west winds which had hampered us so much when
sailing up the west coast in Pen Duick IV. I ought to have had the wind
abeam for this run, and so covered it more quickly.

I eat the last of my smoked salmon for lunch today. I'd hardly dared
hope that it would keep as long as this. It's usually put straight into a
fridge. Mine had gone a little mouldy on the top – but not enough for
it to be thrown overboard.

At 17.30 I finish repairing the first ballooner to get torn.

I've had a very peaceful day with the spi spread from two booms and
the wind astern. In this light breeze the boat has obeyed the self-
steering gear very well, and there's been no fear of her gybing
suddenly. So I've been able to get on with my work.

March 23

At one in the morning the wind shifts forward and I hoist the
mainsail. An hour later I have to take in the spinnaker, and then I run
up the genoa again.

The spi has a tear in it just like the ballooners, but I know the cause
of this. With a swell on, the sail sags down on the boom now and again
and tears itself on the pin holding the boom extension, which is very
sharp. I shall have to wrap some canvas round it.

This morning I might sight the ocean weather ship at point N. I
haven't been trying to follow a course that would take me near this
ship, but have kept heading in the best direction for progressing to the
south-west and the Trade Winds. So it's just by chance if I do sight her.
Usually these weather ships drift over an area of fifteen square miles,
but are supposed to remain within an area three miles square. When a
ship is carried beyond this square, she starts up her engine
and sails back into the wind to the other side of the square, then lets
herself drift again. I'm on a course which should take me slightly
south of point N. At about 10.30 I sight a white vessel on my star-

board bow. The vessel isn't moving, so is very likely the weather ship.

11.30. I am passing about a mile to the south of her. If she had been at the northern edge of her area I might not have sighted her.

At 17.30 I finish stitching the spinnaker, which leaves just one ballooner to mend.

The wind freshens steadily during the evening, and at 21.30 I change the genoa for the No 1 jib.

March 24

At 03.00 I take two reefs in the mainsail. While I am doing this, the wind hauls right round from west to east, which puts the boat on a north-east course. I quickly go about, and so am back on the right course with the wind on the quarter. It is starting to rain.

At 08.00 I let out the two reefs, and as the wind keeps easing I change the No 1 jib for the genoa an hour later.

At 15.00 I have to run up the jib again. The weather has turned squally and the wind strength keeps varying. In these conditions the boat does not respond very well to the self-steering gear, and I have to keep adjusting the tiller.

I've not been able to take a sight today. The sky was clouded over this morning, and although there were a few bright intervals in the afternoon the boat was being buffeted and there was too much spray for using the sextant.

March 25

Because of the gusting wind, it was four in the morning before I went below. It has steadied now, and I can get some sleep. It is blowing at twenty-five knots and I am close hauled on a south-south-westerly course. I ought to be picking up the Trades soon, but this west-south-west wind is a poor substitute.

18.30. A heavy squall and I decide to take in a reef. While getting myself a meal I have great difficulty in boiling the spaghetti – the water won't stay in the saucepan. I'd have done better to cook something else.

During the evening there are some more heavy squalls.

March 26

At 08.00 I take another reef in the mainsail, as it is now blowing a steady thirty-five knots. The sky has cleared, the sun is shining, and the sea, a pretty blue sea, is covered with very white horses.

As I haven't had a fix since the 23rd, I take a sight of the sun with a plastic sextant that I'd bought in case I lost the other or something went wrong with it. This plastic one is a very rudimentary affair but can stand up to getting wet. My noon fix puts me well below the northern limit of the Trade Winds as shown on the pilot charts.

At 15.30 I let out the reefs. Then the wind shifts forward and I have it abeam, course south-west.

20.00. Am again close hauled, hugging the wind, still on a south-westerly course.

Looking over my stock of eggs, I find a great many cracked. It's not surprising, after the lurching about the other day and this morning too. I wipe the survivors and wrap them carefully in lots of paper, so I think they've nothing to fear now.

March 27

Fine lovely weather, but am still close hauled and on a south-westerly course. And yet I've just crossed the Tropic of Cancer. I didn't find the north-westerlies while sailing down her, and now I'm being robbed of the Trade Wind. If there's a regular wind on which you can count, it's that one. What is it up to?

About midday I ran up the genoa, but at 14.00 I replaced it with the No 1 jib, only to change that for the genoa again just now, at 16.00.

The wind veers aft and I take advantage to edge more to the westward, still close hauled but not too close to the wind, and I gain a little speed. Wind strength is very variable, and this means I have to keep a constant eye on the tiller, for as usual the self-steering gear fails to respond to these changes in wind strength.

The fine sunny weather of the morning has given way to a cloudy sky and rain squalls.

March 28

Have had a hard morning. The wind veered aft, so I set the No 2 spinnaker; then it shifted forward and I had to take in the spi and hoist the big ballooner, though not secured to the boom. Then the wind shifted further forward, and I changed the ballooner for the genoa.

First flying fish. Temperature mounting.

A cargo ship passes to the north, a little too far for me to read the name properly – there are two words, something Victory. When on my beam she sounds her siren, and I wave back. At that distance she would not have heard my little foghorn.

March 29

00.30. Light north-east wind. But still not the Trade Wind. I rig the big spinnaker on the two booms, having hauled down the mainsail, and with the wind on the quarter am heading westward, for I've decided to go no further south. As I haven't yet picked up the Trades, when I'm almost on the latitude of Honolulu, I'm not likely to find them further south. There must be some very unusual meteorological conditions prevailing, which have caused the Trade Winds to vanish from these parts.

Cloudy, stormy weather this morning, with the wind almost dying away at times, so that with this swell the spi sags sorrowfully. There's nothing more distressing than to see this sail, usually such a fine sight, gone completely shapeless and with its folds swaying to the rolling of the boat.

Progress is slow, and is taking me a little more to the south than I like. Until four this afternoon there were frequent squally showers but the wind never really got up, only light variable breezes – very variable. At one time the boat was swung completely round in less than three minutes, with the spinnaker spread all the time. I don't know whether there's an official record for that sort of thing, but it's easily my best.

At about 16.00 a bit of a wind gets up suddenly and the spi is taken aback. I get it in. Then I hoist the mainsail and bring in the port boom in order to run up the genoa. With the wind on the starboard beam I am now sailing almost due west and really moving at last. I unrig the starboard boom and tidy away the spinnaker guys and sheets.

I've been getting on with repairing the second big ballooner. In the past few days I've done yards and yards of stitching and there's still a lot more to do on this sail.

I haven't seen any more flying fish since the one yesterday. There ought to be plenty of them in these waters, but perhaps they're seeking the Trade Winds too.

At 23.00 the wind veers aft and I rig a small ballooner on the starboard side, as the wind has freshened too. Making eight knots now, a real pleasure.

March 30

At 08.00, during a rain squall, the wind shifts forward and I get in the small ballooner. It's a heavy shower, but very welcome in these southern latitudes.

10.30. Set the small ballooner again. The wind is in the north-east now – is it the Trades at last? It's coming from the right direction anyway. Between the squalls it's blowing at about fifteen knots, and the boat is speeding along.

12.30. Rig the big ballooner headsail on the lee boom and lower the mainsail. The boat is better balanced and the self-steering gear functions more evenly. For the first time since the start the boat is planing over the swell, with the speedometer registering ten knots.

The lee boom dips in the water now and again, and I'm going to raise it a little.

The headsail isn't so well spread now, but it doesn't dip so often or so much. And otherwise something might break, the downhaul or the lift, which could cause other damage.

At 17.00 the wind hardens and I have to take the helm, as the self-steering gear isn't sufficient by itself.

Lots of flying fish about now, but quite different from the first one I saw. These are much larger and have reddish fins, a very pretty sight.

11

Planing over
the waves

March 31

I've hardly left the helm since yesterday afternoon. Wind still strong. At 00.30 the big ballooner was ripped, torn away at the clew. There was too much wind for it. I've obviously been wrong to have these headsails made of such light material. But to tell the truth I hadn't thought of keeping them spread in such a strong breeze; however, I noticed the boat carried it all right. Another disadvantage of this thin material is that when rolling up the sail the wind presses it tight and I never manage to get more than half of it rolled up, so many turns are needed. Also, I find difficulty in getting in the telescopic boom. The lowest position of the slide on the mast is too high in relation to the height of the support on the pulpit, so that the boom slants down-wards. When there's a swell on, the fore part of the boom reaches the level of the water, and if extended to its full length it dips nine or ten feet into the water. This could have been remedied if there had been more time for trials. The pressure of the water has forced the slide up the mast and shifted the boom from its prop on the pulpit – and there it is dipping almost vertically over the side. Luckily the downhaul is holding and preventing it from moving backwards and hitting against the shrouds, otherwise more damage might have been caused, especi-ally to the crosstrees.

I let go the sheet of the headsail secured to the starboard boom, so that it starts flapping; the boat is almost stopped, and I can get in my boom.

This is the sort of little detail that makes life complicated, and it's to avoid nuisances of this kind that proper trials are so necessary.

I run up the genoa on the port side. The squalls are becoming more frequent and stronger. There are often gusts of thirty knots. The boat is planing over the water nearly all the time. When she gives a spurt the relative wind is coming no more than fifteen degrees abaft the beam, and yet she is almost upright in the water, with the ballast tanks empty. Before planing she is heeled slightly, but then as she gathers speed she planes almost upright, very quickly, with a bow wave reaching level with the mast. Once she's started planing, there's no trouble about steering. But there is before.

There's an unusually confused sea and now and again helm has to be applied vigorously. Three times the boat shoots into the wind and heels over at an alarming angle. There's just time to say quickly, 'I know you can't capsize, I know . . .' three times, and at that moment the weather ballooner is taken aback, the boat swings round like a top, the ballooner billows out suddenly and off we go again. All in the space of a few seconds. So no time is lost.

Unfortunately, the third time this happens, the ballooner is ripped right across. With my limited equipment, I shall never be able to repair it. I regret more than ever not having these sails made of stronger material. I've only just picked up the Trades, and already half the sails are unusable. A fine outcome. I must try to go easy with the others.

With only the genoa set, the boat responds nicely to the self-steering gear. Speed must have dropped by about one and a half knots. I seize the opportunity to take a noonday sight (noon by local time, but I have kept San Francisco time), have an hour's sleep and then eat. I plotted my position and see that I have run 193 nautical miles in twenty-four hours, which gives an average of eight knots.

Instead of risking a ballooner, which I'm now treasuring for light breezes, I run up the No 1 jib already broken out and secure it to the boom, then take the helm. I luff as much as I can with the jib up, as my midday fix shows that I shall soon pass fairly close to the north of Kauai Island, the northernmost of the Hawaii Islands.

I was lucky to have been able to get a fix at midday, for the sky clouded over soon afterwards. When near land it is useful to know your position on the chart.

18.00. In this thick weather it is impossible to sight the island, and I ought to have done so long ago, as it's very high. I'm not at all sure of having passed it, so I'm going to take in the No 1 jib to be able to luff. That's safer, as in this breeze it would be unpleasant to have to luff while almost close hauled, if the island suddenly loomed in sight. A pity, because the boat's sailing really fast, making about nine knots nearly all the time and planing in an amazing manner, the relative wind coming almost abeam. The average speed must be over ten knots. There's a lot of strain on the tiller, but planing like this is quite amusing.

To take in the jib I had to lower both sails at once, as one of the jib's hanks had got caught on the stay while the sail was flapping. I ran up the genoa again and sighted the island just at that moment. I could have cleared it by maintaining course, but in any case I did the right thing. These jibs with hanks are not meant to be hoisted broken out, and when they flap the hanks catch at everything and get buckled.

Under the genoa alone, speed is comparatively slow, and the self-steering gear is not acting because the boat is not well balanced. I pump some water into the starboard tank and hoist the mainsail with a reef in it. The self-steering gear works no better. I take in the genoa and run up the No 1 jib, secure it to the stay and the starboard boom. That's a lot better – the boat zigzags a little but sails really fast, planing magnificently over the water. I hope to be able to go and eat and then sleep in peace.

April 1

I took the helm very early, having let out the reef in the mainsail to increase speed even more. Wind still very strong, but the sun has been out all day.

I took a sight at midday, and I've run exactly 240 miles in twenty-four hours. There's a favourable one knot current, so that leaves nine knots for the boat. As she slowed down a lot when I was not at the helm, she must have been making an average of ten knots most of the time I was at the tiller. That's very fast for a boat of this size.

The flying fish are back to normal – perhaps those I saw with reddish fins are special to the waters around Hawaii.

April 2

Wind strength has dropped to about twenty knots. Lovely weather. There is not such a heavy sea as yesterday.

At midday I set the small ballooner on the port boom, the lee side. It's the only one of the four ballooners fit for use. Should I take in the mainsail? For the moment, speed has increased. With the wind on the quarter, these two sails seem to be drawing very well, so I'll keep the mainsail up.

14.00. I change the No 1 jib, on the weather side, for the genoa.

April 3

There's a very large creature accompanying the boat this morning. It's at least twenty feet long. I thought at first it might be a killer whale, but then I remembered that they never surface in order to blow. This is a splendid creature, streamlined and with a sparkling white belly that I get a glimpse of when it turns on its back. Possibly a tiger shark. Sometimes it swims along just astern of me, sometimes it precedes the boat, so that it keeps dropping back or flashing past. When it's astern, now and again I can see this elongated body glinting just below the white crests of the swell, illuminated by the sun. It kept me company for more than an hour. A lovely sight.

tamponné sous le vent à bâbord. c'est le seul en état sur les quatre. Faut-il ou non amener la grand'voile ? Pour l'instant on a accéléré. Grand largue, près du travers les deux voiles ont l'air de bien travailler et je la garde.

14 heures je tamponne le génois à la place du foc n° 1 au vent

Le 3 avril. Le matin je vois une grosse bête près du bateau qui fait route avec moi. Ça fait au minimum 6 ou 7 mètres de long aussi je pense d'abord qu'il s'agit d'un orque. C'est une bête magnifique, très profilé avec un ventre d'une blancheur éclatante que je vois quand elle se met sur le dos. De temps en temps elle est derrière et à d'autres moments devant se laissant rattraper ou au contraire me dépassant comme une flèche. Quand elle est derrière moi je la vois quelquefois ce long fuseau au sommet de la houle juste sous la crête blanche et éclairé par transparence par le soleil qui est derrière. C'est vraiment un beau spectacle. Plus tard en en faisant la description à des spécialistes j'apprendrai qu'il s'agit d'un requin tigre. Ce n'était pas le bon endroit pour se baigner. Il va naviguer avec moi pendant plus d'une heure.

Et 11 heures j'amène la grand'voile qui avait

83 A page from Tabarly's log

At 11.00 I take in the mainsail as the boat is inclined to luff. This is an opportunity to mend one of the batten pockets.

My midday position shows me to be only ninety miles from the longitude which is the halfway mark.

April 4

Have passed the halfway mark. Finished repairing the big ballooner headsail – ouf! The other one is too badly torn and repairing it would be too complicated for me to make a sound job of it, so I shan't attempt it. So I'm left with one large and one small ballooner.

At 23.00 I half fill the starboard ballast tanks, then take the helm as the wind has hardened.

April 5

During the night I caught my first flying fish. I often found several flying fish on deck in the morning when sailing Pen Duick IV in the Trade Wind zone, but Pen Duick V doesn't seem very good at catching them. Probably because she's too low in the water and also because there's very little bulwark to retain the fish once they land on deck. It's sheer bad luck for this one to have ended up on board. I heard it whizz past my head, and then it smacked into the mainsail which was furled round the boom and got trapped inside a fold. I heard it flopping about for a little while, then I went and tossed it into the cockpit. It's a good size and I'm hoping to have fish to eat today.

I've been skimming along very fast all night, planing very often and in a spectacular manner in these phosphorescent waters – as they often are in the tropics. The bows send showers of sparkling spray to fall glistening on the deck, while astern there is a wide luminous sheet of water in the boat's wake. The wind is not very steady but still remains strong between the rain squalls – then it increases to quite thirty knots, and each wave is like rolling surf.

In the morning there is a lot of cloud about and it keeps raining on and off. Then the wind steadies and the strength stays around thirty knots.

No sun at midday, so I can't take a sight, but this doesn't matter from a navigational point of view (where I am it's of no consequence to go forty-eight hours without a fix), yet I should have liked to know what the average speed has been in the past twenty-four hours, as the boat seems to have travelled very fast.

When night falls I have been at the helm for twenty hours, and with the long time spent in the cockpit a few days ago, my back and my bottom ache like anything. I think I'll take in the ballooner and hoist the mainsail, then change the genoa set on the weather boom for the No 1 jib.

That done, the boat responds to the self-steering gear and I can go and get something to eat, for I'm starving. My flying fish, alas, has to be thrown away. It's been lying in the cockpit all day and never been gutted, so with this heat it's hardly likely to be eatable. I shall have scrambled eggs instead. That's the quickest, and I'm longing to lie down.

April 6

I had two hours sleep four times last night. I've two means of waking up from time to time to see how things are. One is to set the course indicator, which makes a hell of a din with its horn whenever the boat goes too much off course. This is the better way, as then I'm wakened each time I need to be and only when I need to be. The alarm goes off when the wind direction changes or even when the strength changes. With the defective self-steering gear, each wind variation affects the boat's course. But that apart, a change in wind strength which calls for a shortening of canvas is noticeable from inside the cabin, without any need of an alarm. A boat carrying too much canvas rouses her skipper by the change in heel and the sounds of the water. And if the wind eases so much that more sail is required, then here again the skipper is very likely to become aware of it while sleeping, so much is his unconscious mind affected by all the sounds made by the boat.

However, with an alarm he can be absolutely sure of waking – especially with one like mine. Its horn is so noisy and the pitch so unpleasant that it would drag the laziest person from his bunk, all the more so as it doesn't stop until the boat is back on course. The disadvantage is, being an electric apparatus run off the one and only battery on board, I have to be very sparing in my use of it, as I need to have current available until the finish of the race. So I set this alarm only when the winds are variable, as was often the case before picking up the Trades.

When I do not set it I use instead an ordinary alarm clock, which I place close to my bunk and set it to wake me in an hour or an hour and a half, according to the weather conditions prevailing. Last night, as I badly needed a rest, I set the alarm for two hours. The wind was steady and there were no signs of a change in the offing, so I could sleep easy.

This morning I change the No 1 jib for the genoa again. The wind has eased a little and the boat responds better to the self-steering gear, but it still cannot be relied upon. I spend a good part of the day at the helm.

When I plot my position at midday I see that I've crossed the international date line, longitude 180. So I ought to advance the day's date and this entry in my log ought to be dated the 7th instead of the 6th. Then there wouldn't be a 6th. As one can see from the diagram (84) representing the equator, or any parallel, that while it is 10.00 hours on April 6 for me on longitude 180, it's 22.00 on April 6 on Greenwich meridian and also 10.00 on April 7 on longitude 180. It's the April 6 for me on one side of the line and April 7 as soon as I've crossed it. So as one travels west from the meridian one ought to put one's watch back an hour when crossing a time zone, and eventually this is compensated for by advancing the date by twenty-four hours on crossing longitude 180. This necessity to change the date is probably

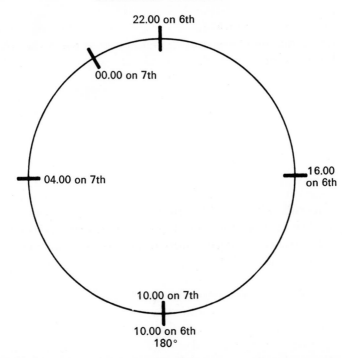

more easily understood by taking the example of a plane flying westward at a speed equal to the earth's rotation. The speed would not be much flying round near one of the Poles; the pilot puts his watch back one hour as he crosses a time zone, but as it will have taken him an hour's flying time he puts his watch back to what it was originally. If he starts his flight at 12.00, his watch shows 13.00 on crossing a time zone, and he puts it back to 12.00. This can go on indefinitely. He can fly round near the Pole a great many times, and for him it will still be noon. He doesn't get any older. If he remains in the air while the earth rotates three times, when he lands he will be three days behind the calendar. But if he advances the date by one day each time he crosses longitude 180, then he will be up to date when he lands.

However, for my part, today will remain the 6th. What interests me is the number of days at sea since the start of the race. I'll change the date after reaching the finish.

At 18.00, in order to balance the boat better, I set the No 1 jib on the lee boom and lower the mainsail.

April 7
The wind drops in the early morning but I wait a little before

84   Greenwich meridian

increasing sail, as there is a heavy black cloud coming up. But it only brings rain, the wind doesn't get up again, so I start to change the No 1 jib for the small ballooner. While lowering the jib I see that a strand of the halyard has split. I hesitate about mending it at once. My first thought is that the halyard is still strong enough to take the strain of the ballooner, especially in this light wind, and that while I'm making an eye splice the boat will be deprived of this sail and have her speed reduced a bit. However, on second thoughts, I decide to do the job there and then. It should only take about an hour, so little distance will be lost. The weather is calm, I can work in good conditions. Whereas if I left it till later, the wind might get up again and I should be obliged to take in the sail for fear the halyard broke completely; and the job would take longer in those unfavourable conditions. So I get out the tools, cut the halyard where it's worn and splice the two ends together. This shortens the halyard by about three feet, but I always take care to have them overlong. They nearly always wear at the same place, near the head.

At the end of the morning the wind strength increases and the boat speeds along again.

At 13.00 the wind eases again and veers aft. It continues to shift as fast as I trim the sails. I gybe, and when I'm on the other tack the wind hauls forward until the headsails are no longer drawing. I hoist the mainsail. I take in the ballooner and remove the boom of the genoa, which is now on the lee side. The wind is abeam now, and as it is easing again I spread the big spinnaker. Hardly have I done this than the wind veers aft. I rig a second boom for the spi, and I lower the mainsail.

It's a roundabout of handling. But that is not the end of this day's gymnastics. When the big spinnaker is rigged on two booms, for it to be well spread the halyard needs to be slackened off by about five feet. And now, in this swell, the spinnaker's rising and falling motion eventually flips the halyard over the head of the wind direction indicator fixed to the top of the mast. The head is bent downwards and the pointer has been wrenched off. The halyard is getting caught almost every time the boat pitches, and it's a wonder that the rotor of the wind speed indicator hasn't been wrenched off too. I shall have to climb up and get the apparatus down, for it costs a lot of money. Perhaps the head isn't broken.

I get it down, and now I'm without a very useful piece of equipment.

After that, the wind shifts forward and I hoist the mainsail again. At 20.00 it veers aft again, and I lower the mainsail. The wind hardens but is still variable; I can see I shall have to keep adjusting the tiller, so instead of going below I shall take cat-naps on a sail bag below the hatch.

April 8

This is the loveliest day since the start. A fifteen knot wind and glorious sunshine, and am speeding along with the wind on the quarter. I'm able to do some tidying up, and I connect the fresh water pump – something there wasn't time to do before the start, nor since. It's very convenient though; instead of having to fill a jerrican and carry it to the sink, now there's water straight from the tap. But priorities have to be established for these jobs, and there were always others to be done that were more urgent. Perhaps they'll all get done by the time I reach the finish.

This evening I come to the end of my banana diet. The whole supply ripened more or less at the same time, so that for the past five days I've been eating nothing but bananas. The evening meal has consisted of just one course of six or seven *bananes flambées*. It wasn't terribly good the first time, but the second attempt was better and after the third the dish was just about perfect.

The pineapples are finished too. But I still have some oranges and lemons, apples, cucumbers and onions, all in excellent condition.

The wind tonight looks like being as variable as it was last night, so I shall take cat-naps again or stay on watch.

I make use of the time by learning the names of the stars with the help of my book.

April 9

During the morning there was stormy weather and a freshening wind, so I have to take the helm again. In the afternoon the storms pass over but the wind stays strong and I remain at the helm, the wind being right aft. At the end of the afternoon the wind moderates and I can engage the self-steering gear.

I shall be able to go below and get some sleep tonight, setting the alarm clock to go off every hour.

April 10

Wakened at 05.00 – I thought the wind must have dropped completely, as I could hear no splashing. But on going on deck I see the spinnaker flapping like a flag. The starboard sheet had broken away – the snap shackle had come open and the sail was torn at that edge. In this light wind and with a swell on, the spi must have got blown against the end of the boom and torn itself. I get it in, and set the small ballooner on the port side and the large one on the starboard. I start mending the spi straight away.

I take a sight at midday, and I judge from my position that the time has come to alter course from due west to north-west, to head up for Tokyo. I have another 1,600 miles to go. I've sailed 4,100 in twenty-six days, which gives an average speed of 6.6 knots. I hope to reach the finish in another eleven days, which would make a total of thirty-seven.

During the afternoon I repair the lifeline I broke yesterday. It almost caused me to fall overboard, as it gave way while I was leaning against it. It's a stranded steel wire with a plastic casing, and the ends have been coupled without removing the casing. This makes for a neater job, as when the casing is not taken up in the coupling it eventually shrinks a little and the bare wire appears at the ends. On the other hand, the plastic casing prevents the wire strands from being pressed tight by the coupling sleeve, and the cable becomes loose inside the casing. It's a fault that would never have occurred to me, but now that I know about it I shall take heed in future.

April 11

Wind right aft, light breeze. The hottest day so far. Making very little speed. In these conditions my ballooners aren't too light, and as there happens to be a flat sea they don't flap too much. The sea is a deep blue, with small wavelets sparkling in the sun.

Towards the end of the afternoon a merchantship coming up astern alters course slightly to pass close. But as there happens to be a little more wind and the boat is making six knots, by the time the ship overhauls me it is almost dark. She passes very close, and I light my big lamp to be sure of her seeing me. She slips past a few yards distant . . . making me feel very small and I think that it isn't the moment for her helmsman to make a mistake. It is too dark for me to make out her name.

April 12

During the night the light breeze gradually dies down, and at 02.00 the ballooners are suddenly taken aback. I lower them, hoist the mainsail, bring in the booms and then run up the genoa.

In the next two hours there are several thunderstorms and the wind keeps shifting and varying in strength. At about 07.00 it steadies from the north but is very, very light. The boat is making half a knot.

At 10.00, flat calm. At 11.00, a little breeze from the north-north-east. I set the big ballooner as a ghoster. It fills and draws all right, whereas the genoa is flapping all the time in this swell.

Five pilot fish are escorting me, two large and three small ones. They keep darting at any little thing to see if it's edible. I've never seen these fish before.

12.00. The wind veers aft and I set the medium spinnaker. At 13.30 the wind freshens and shifts forward. I run up the light genoa. Am close hauled, on course and making seven knots. This is the best of weather.

At 19.00 the breeze hardens and I change the light genoa for the heavy one. Speed is eight knots.

About 10.30 the wind eases and veers aft. I set the spi and speed increases from six to seven knots.

At the end of the day the wind eases a little more, and at 21.00 I take in the spi so that I can go below and eat and then sleep for a bit. Although I intended to set the spi again at about four in the morning if weather conditions were still the same, I did not leave the boom rigged in case I had to alter my plans.

April 14

At 00.30 my alarm rouses me from a good sleep. The boat is on a northerly course. The wind has shifted to the east, and on this course I have it abaft the beam. The spinnaker is indicated, so I set it and take the tiller.

At 07.00 the wind veers right aft, I rig the second boom and lower the mainsail. A little later I gybe, the wind having veered south-south-east. But it's very light. Speed is between four and five knots.

My position at midday shows that I've 980 miles to go. It's comforting to come down to three figures.

There's almost a flat calm in the afternoon, in fact it is completely calm at times. Average speed during the afternoon, two knots.

A little breeze gets up in the evening and speed increases to five knots.

April 15

At 02.00 the wind veers south-south-west. I trim the spi for this beam wind and take the helm. At 04.00 the wind shifts forward and I have to take in the spi. The boat is under mainsail and light genoa in this very variable wind.

At 10.30 the wind shifts further forward and I am now close hauled and well off course – whichever tack I go on, It's blowing dead from the north-west. I might have expected this, as the pilot chart shows north-westerly winds as having the lowest percentage of all for the area I am in.

Becalmed throughout the afternoon. In the evening a little breeze gets up from the south-west, but is very fluky.

I was wakened about every twenty minutes during the night by the horn of the course indicator going off. To remain more or less on course I had to keep trimming the sails, being either close hauled or on a reach.

April 16

04.00 Becalmed again. It's as though the nearer I get to the finish, the slower my progress becomes.

08.00. A breeze gets up from the south-east. I rig the spinnaker on two booms and lower the mainsail. Now making four knots.

Wind veers south-south-west. I trim the spi for this beam wind and hoist the mainsail again. Speed five then six knots. Sea quite flat, lovely weather, very comfortable sailing. Temperature still high, but there's a feel of heading northwards.

At 13.00 the breeze freshens, am making seven knots. At 14.00, eight knots, but then I have to take the helm.

At 20.00 the wind shifts forward and I get in the spi. While doing this, the wind hardens and so speed is maintained under the genoa.

April 17

Since 04.00 wind strength has been steadily increasing. The barometer is going down. At 07.00 I change the genoa for the No.1 jib.

The weather becomes very overcast during the morning, and a drizzle sets in. Real Breton sou'westerly weather. The wind strength is twenty-five knots. At midday it suddenly veers west-north-west. I go on the starboard tack, this being slightly more favourable, about ten degrees closer to my course. At the same time the wind eases considerably, and the boat is labouring in a lumpy sea, a result of the south-westerly wind.

At 16.00 I run up the genoa. The wind veers aft at about 17.30 – I'm almost dead on course and speed is five knots. Barometer rising again.

April 18

All night the wind has been very light, dying to nothing half the time. When there was a wind its strength was very variable, so that I had to keep adjusting the tiller, and it varied in direction too, sometimes by as much as forty degrees. So I was awake all night – and all for twenty-five miles! I've rarely sailed through an area with such fluky winds.

Practically becalmed all morning. A little flurry now and again enables me to progress five miles in four hours. and even then not always in the right direction.

At 14.30 a wind at last gets up from the west, and I am making five and half knots and am nearly three points off course. The pilot chart forecasts one per cent of calms for this area! I certainly have a knack of finding different conditions from those given on these charts.

At 15.00 the wind drops, but gets up again at 18.00. By 20.00 it is time to set the heavy genoa, but at 21.30 I change it for the No.1 jib.

April 19

At 01.30 I run into a heavy squall. There are thick storm clouds about and the wind strength is thirty knots. So I take two reefs in the mainsail, but while doing this the winds shifts forward and puts me on a northerly course. I go about, to make westing. When the wind is as strong as this I wear round in order to shift the ballast from one pair of tanks to the other while I have the wind on the quarter. In this way there's no difficulty over the operation.

I thought it was just a squall and that the wind would drop again. But nothing of the kind – the storm has passed over, the sky has cleared, but the wind is even stronger – thirty-five knots. So at 06.00 I run up the No. 2 jib.

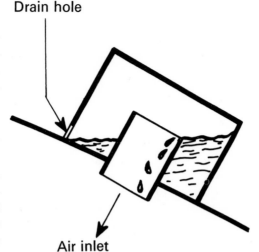

Drain hole

Air inlet

85   Leaking ventila

With the boat heeling over a lot, about thirty degrees, water has come in through the ventilators on to the bunks. The deflector has a drainage hole only on one side (85), so that when the boat heels a lot the other way, the water rises to the level of the air inlet. Another small detail needing to be put right, and which becomes obvious only through sailing the boat.

The Force 8 wind held all day and the sea heaped up and became rough and disturbed. However, I was making headway, which was preferable to being becalmed. I kept enough canvas set to maintain speed this time, however much the boat got banged about. And there was plenty of that. Each wave made her shudder all over and she seemed to be trying to disintegrate. When I stretched out in my bunk the banging sounds went through my head and I began to feel quite ill. In conditions like these, life aboard is far from pleasant.

At about 17.00 the wind begins to ease. It veers aft too, so that I'm now back on course and close hauled, full and bye.

At 23.00 I set the heavy genoa.

April 20

At 06.00 I let out the reefs in the mainsail, then set the light genoa.

During the morning the wind again eases and becomes rather light, so that I'm doing little better than crawling along. No doubt about it, there's no happy medium in this area of the ocean, either the wind is too strong or else there's not enough. But it's a lovely day, and I take the opportunity to go below armed with hammer and chisel to make another drain hole in the ventilator deflectors. So now I hope my bunks will stay dry whatever the weather.

The wind falls away early in the afternoon so I set the big ballooner to ghost along. I manage to make three knots nevertheless.

April 21

01.00. The wind veers right aft, and I rig the big spinnaker on its two booms, then lower the mainsail. Soon afterwards I have to gybe, then to luff until I have the wind abeam. In a couple of hours the wind has hauled right round.

I hoist the mainsail again. At 06.00, with the wind shifting forward again, I get in the spi and set the genoa. Another night of low mileage.

But now a breeze has got up and I'm moving fast again. The wind shifts forward too, and at 09.00 I'm sailing full and bye.

I notice this morning that there's a distinct change in the colour of the water. The clear Pacific blue has given way to a greenish hue.

In the afternoon the weather becomes overcast and the wind freshens.

April 22

02.00. No1 jib again – squally weather with a gusting wind, and it's raining.

At 09.00 I run up the genoa. The wind is easing all the time and becomes very light. It also shifts forward, so that I'm now heading north. Of course, in this area the lowest percentage of winds comes from the west, according to the pilot chart . . . I might have known!

At 11.00, with the wind still shifting forward, I go on the other tack. Then the wind gradually veers aft and by midday I am on course again. Soon afterwards I ease the sheets and with the freshening wind abeam am making three and a half knots instead of the two this morning. Speed even increases to five knots, and this is kept up all afternoon.

I must now be in the Kuro Shiwo, or Black Stream (86–91), the current which flows along this coast of Japan in a south-west to north-east direction. The main current sometimes flows at more than two knots, which was not to be ignored. As I was approaching it from the south-east, seemingly I had but to cross it at right angles while making leeway. But unfortunately this current meanders quite a lot and keeps shifting in an unpredictable manner. In order for the competitors to have some idea of this phenomenon, the race organizers had given us diagrams showing the behaviour of the current. It could be seen that, on the whole, the behaviour of this Kuro Shiwo current is not unlike that of the Gulf Stream, whose general direction and average speed are known but which wanders about and keeps shifting.

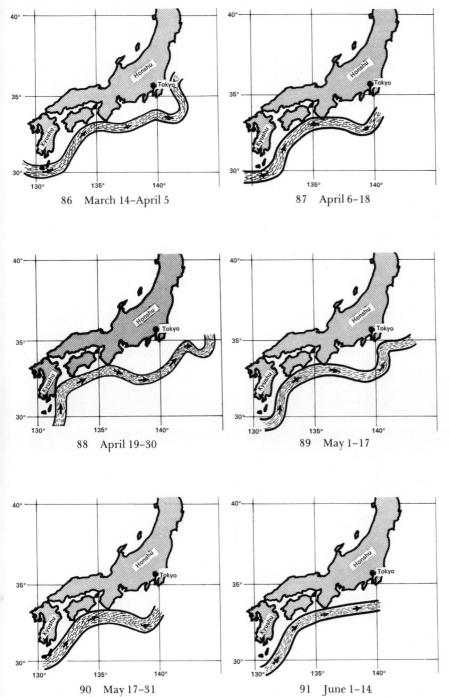

86   March 14–April 5

87   April 6–18

88   April 19–30

89   May 1–17

90   May 17–31

91   June 1–14

86–91   The Japanese
Current 1968 (Black
Stream or Kuro Siwo)

On studying these diagrams I had observed that on approaching the bay of Tokyo from the south-east I was likely to find myself in the current flowing more or less as it had been between March 14 and April 5, 1968, in which case it would be against me. But if I made course for the position 33 degrees north 141 degrees east I might well avoid having the current against me, in fact it might be favourable for carrying me towards the finish if it were flowing as shown on the diagram (89) for May 1–17. So I had made for that position, and am now quite close to it.

At about 13.00 I pass through some debris which is almost certainly the sign of a current. I began to make leeway. The sea is much more choppy than it should be, indicating that the current is flowing against the wind – highly probable, as the wind is north-north-east. About 18.00 I reach an area where the waters are literally boiling, with foam cresting the waves although the wind is very light. This lasts about an hour, while I am probably passing through the main flow. I notice a few flying fish – it's many days since I last saw any.

I'm getting near the finishing line now; and with this current, whose strength and direction are doubtful making dead reckoning problematical, I need to navigate accurately if I'm not to miss my landfall and sail farther than is necessary. So this evening I take a sight of the stars. The leeway I made must have been about right, for I'm well on course.

The breeze keeps easing and by 23.00 there's a flat calm.

April 23

Becalmed all night. A great amount of dew. The sun rises on a perfectly smooth sea, a sea of glass. If things continue like this I shan't even get to the finish today.

At ten a little breeze gets up from the west, and I start my finishing sprint at one and a half knots. I've just sighted a cargo vessel, the first for quite a time. She passes well astern of me, heading south-west.

Throughout the morning I remain close hauled but on course, making one and a half or two knots. Just before midday the wind freshens a little and veers aft until I have it abeam. I set the big ballooner as a ghoster and speed increases to three knots.

After taking a noon sight I'm pleasantly surprised to find that I've only sixty miles to go. Since plotting my position yesterday evening, the current has taken me twenty miles or so in the right direction. It must be flowing much as it was during the period May 1–17 last year.

The weather is lovely, and in the early afternoon the wind freshens. By 14.00 the boat is making eight knots, she knows she's heading for harbour. It's a long time since she skimmed along like this.

Later in the afternoon I check my course. There's a mist all along the horizon and visibility can't be more than five miles. So I shan't sight land until the last moment, and need to be on the right bearing.

16.30. Just made my landfall. It's the southern headland of the bay of Tokyo, slightly to leeward of me. Now I have to round it quite close to head for the finishing line, which is under the northern headland.

The wind is freshening again, so I change the ballooner for the genoa. I can now see a lot of coastal shipping ahead, and as night falls their navigation lights are all around me. There is still a good breeze, and I make a dash for the finish at nine or ten knots, a sort of slalom between the coastal vessels. As they are tagging along one behind the other, in both directions, I'm happy to have speed on in order to cross their paths, especially as my own lights aren't working.

The finishing line is marked by a small red light called I-Sa which is positioned west of the island of Zyo-ga-Sa. I have to sail to the west of I-Sa, and shall have crossed the line when I sight the light to the east. This I do at 20.59 – which is 03.59 on April 24 by San Francisco time. So I have taken 39 days 15 hours 44 minutes. Average speed was six knots.

12
Victory without a judge

As soon as I crossed the finishing line I took in the genoa and made for the small harbour of Misaki, as competitors had been instructed to do by the race organizers. We had been told that the judges' boat would be moored in the middle of the harbour and that we should report our arrival to them. I entered the harbour and sailed round it under mainsail but saw no sign of the judges' boat. I was not worried by this, for the instructions took account of the probability of a competitor finishing at a time when the judges' boat would not be out in the harbour, and in such an event the competitor was to go to the small museum near the Zyo-ga-Sa lighthouse and contact the attendant, who would phone the Nippon Ocean Racing Club, the organizing body at this end of the race.

I found a berth along the quay and tied up, took down the mainsail and went below to sleep without fear of having to turn out again half an hour or so later. It was the daylight that woke me. I had a good breakfast, eating it leisurely in the cockpit and being pleasantly warmed by the sun, which was already well up. There was no sign of life anywhere along the quay. At about seven I went ashore. The village still seemed to be asleep, the streets were empty as I strolled along looking about me. It was much as I had imagined a Japanese village to be – there were quite small houses studding the hillside in haphazard fashion, joined by winding streets too narrow for a car to pass. But the houses themselves, except for their smallness, were rather different from what I had imagined; instead of wood and bamboo, with stiff paper for glass in the windows, the chief building materials were cement and galvanised iron. Most of the houses I saw were also little restaurants or shops selling groceries, fish, and holiday souvenirs, from which I concluded that this part of the coast must be very popular.

Then I saw my first Japanese – a man opening up his shop. I was wondering just what the local time was, and I tried to make him understand what I wanted to know by sign language and pointing to my watch – which still showed San Francisco time. He eventually grasped what I was after and showed me his clock. The time was as I thought, a quarter past seven. The museum would not be open yet, but I continued walking in the direction of the lighthouse to find where it was. The streets began to show signs of life. I reached the lighthouse by a path skirting the shore. There were big jagged rocks and a strong smell of seaweed; I might have been in Brittany. But there is very little tide here, five feet at most. I looked in vain for a museum in the neighbourhood of the lighthouse; nothing had any resemblance to one, and although there were some notices they were of no help to me, being entirely in Japanese.

It was then after eight, so this museum might be open; at any rate, I could ask someone. I approached several people, but none of them spoke a word of French or English. I was beginning to despair when along came a group of boys and girls in school uniform. One of their monitors knew a little English, and she showed me the museum, which was a museum about lighthouses. The attendant spoke only Japanese, nevertheless on seeing me he ought to have guessed what I had come about – if the race organizers had informed him of his role.

The girl and most of the others had followed me in, and I tried to explain to her what I wanted so that she could interpret for me. I repeated that I was one of the competitors in a sailing race from San Francisco, and at last got her to understand. She told the others, who until then had just been staring curiously and with some amusement at my month-old beard and torn jeans; now they gathered round, chattering among themselves and looking at me with interest. I pulled my printed instructions from my pocket and pointed to the one concerning arrival procedure for the girl to read it. After about ten attempts, and aided by explanations from me, she finally got the gist of it and started to tell the attendant. As though by a miracle, a few minutes later I was talking over the phone to the secretary of the Nippon Ocean Racing Club. He said they had not expected anyone to arrive so soon, and he congratulated me. He would at once inform the Customs and Immigration so that the formalities could be completed as soon as possible. I was to return on board and wait for the officials.

So I went back to Pen Duick V, and soon afterwards the officials arrived. They each filled up several forms, and that was that. A few minutes later a launch brought the manager of the marina where a berth was retained for Pen Duick V. The marina was in a cove quite close at hand, I understood. He came aboard and I got under way. It was a well sheltered cove with steep, wooded banks, and was one of the few places in the region where craft were safe from typhoons. As soon as a typhoon is forecast, all the small fishing vessels of the area come and take shelter in this cove, which is then packed to the limit. The marina was well inside the cove, with lines of mooring for boats.

A hot bath was soon ready for me in the clubhouse. I was told that this custom of taking very hot baths was the reason for the soft skin of the Japanese. For lunch I was given a Japanese speciality – *shoushis,* small balls of rice and raw fish that you pick up with chopsticks and dip in *shoyu* sauce. They are very tasty, and I recommend them all the more gladly as I had little liking for the seaweed dishes that the Japanese like. After lunch I was interviewed by reporters, nearly all of whom thoughtfully turned up at the same time and so simplified matters.

A few days later I visited Tokyo, a huge city, perhaps the biggest in the world; but I found little that was attractive about it. The few modern districts have no originality and are surrounded by what appears to be one huge village with narrow streets and small houses extending as far as the eye can see. Many streets have motorways built above them, so that the traffic is at roof level. I suppose it's one way of solving the traffic problem, but to my mind is practicable only if there's nothing below worth preserving. I don't think I should like to see Paris subjected to such sorry methods of town planning.

From Aburatsubo, where Pen Duick V was berthed, I set sail to spend the weekend on the island of O-Sima, at the mouth of the bay of Tokyo, taking with me as guide and crew a Frenchman who lived in Tokyo. This island is in fact a volcano. The harbour where we put in has been created from an extinct crater by simply blowing a gap in the edge bordering the sea – and now there is this circular harbour surrounded by steep cliffs and with a narrow entrance. Inland, the main crater is still active. We climbed up to the top and stood looking down into the smoking depths.

On my return on the Monday morning I had a great surprise. Among the sailing craft manoeuvring in the bay was one changing jibs, and the new jib was red. This roused my curiosity, for there can't be many jibs of that colour – was it Jean-Yves Terlain by any chance? I looked through my binoculars. Indeed it was! I changed tack to go and greet him. I went alongside and told him that he was second and congratulated him on having beaten Claus Hehner, who had the faster boat. It was a fine performance. He wanted to know how I had got on, and I said that I had arrived ten days ago. Meeting him like that was an amazing coincidence.

In Japan the sea is never very far away. The main island, Hondo, the largest and most populous and the site of most of the cities including Tokyo, has nowhere a width exceeding 250 miles. But I was rather forgetting the mountains, which are quite high and numerous. Two of the French skiing team, Florence Steurer and Patrick Russel, had just arrived in Tokyo, and I spent a few days in the mountains with them and their trainer, Gaston Perrot. My skiing experience is somewhat limited, so despite the excellent advice I was given I didn't make a very good show on the slopes – where the snow was melting – but I enjoyed myself immensely in the company of those friendly athletes.

There was one thing I wanted to do very much before leaving Japan – to sail round the Inland Sea. This Japanese 'Mediterranean' – though much the smaller – is an inlet of the Pacific Ocean and is joined to the Sea of Japan on the west only by the narrow straits of Shimonoseki, being bounded by Hondo to the north and east, by the island of Kiushiu to the west and the island of Shikoku to the south. There are two straits leading from the Pacific, on either side of Shikoku. Ever since arriving in Japan everyone had been telling me how very picturesque it was and how characteristic of the scenery of Japan; and about Kyoto too, the ancient capital, which I ought to visit, and which is some thirty miles inland from Osaka, the big port and industrial centre at the eastern end of the Inland Sea. I had hesitated about going there, for from the bay of Tokyo it meant a cruise of a thousand miles there and back.

But I set sail at midday on May 14. There was a light south-easterly breeze and the weather was lovely. This beam wind freshened during the evening, and once I had passed the Mikomoto Rock and was out of the bay, at about midnight, I was on a westerly course and had the wind on the quarter. I spread the spinnaker and was soon making eight or nine knots. At about ten in the morning a sudden, fierce squall laid the boat over almost horizontally, and so she stayed. Before she could recover I had to go and ease the spi sheet on the lee side, but the sail tore while I was trying to get at it. The split went from near the head of the sail almost to the foot. The boat recovered, and all that remained for me to do was to gather up the debris. I set the genoa on a boom. The squall had passed – it had lasted only a few seconds.

I had another sleepless night, for there was so much coastal shipping that it was impossible to go below. A bay here and there looked quiet and tempting, but I had little time to spare and did not want to heave to.

At about 14.00 on May 16 I put into the small port of Tanabe, from where I intended to take the train to Kyoto. I had been dragging along all morning, having lost the nice breeze as soon as I rounded Shivomisaki Point. I had come 310 miles, which left 140 to reach the Inland Sea by rounding a long peninsula.

Later that afternoon I was in Kyoto, where I was the guest of Mr Sawayama, the French Vice-Consul at Nagasaki. But as that large port and city on the island of Kiushiu is not nearly so pleasant as the ancient capital, he had his residence there despite the long distance from his office. His daughter showed me round Kyoto the following day. It was impossible to see everything in a few hours, but we visited the fine Imperial Palace and some magnificent Shinto temples, such as the Chiou-In which is reached by long flights of stone steps. What I enjoyed most were the gardens and parks with their trees of many varieties, lakes and running water. Those I liked best were the gardens of the Kin-kaku-Ji temple and the Garden of Mosses. In the Garden of Stones there were monks sitting and meditating; the finer aspects of Zen philosophy escape me, but nevertheless I greatly appreciated the peace and quiet of the surroundings.

Late that evening I was back on board Pen Duick V, and set sail with a strong north-westerly dead on the nose. I took a reef in the mainsail and set the No 1 jib. It was past midnight when I left harbour. I had the right canvas for the moment, but this did not last long. An hour later I was taking another reef in the mainsail, and shortly afterwards I changed the No 1 jib for the No 2. There was a Force 8 wind, and as usual in these conditions the boat was slamming like a mad thing. About six in the morning the wind eased suddenly and veered aft, just as I was at the end of a tack and close to the coast. I had taken a drubbing for nothing; if I were just setting sail from Tanabe I shouldn't have been far behind where I now was. It would serve as a lesson for not having had the courage to make short tacks and keep more on course. Fortunately this wasn't a race, and besides if it had been I probably shouldn't have done as I did.

The fine weather held all day, but the wind was very light and I was continually tacking, so it was the following morning before I entered the Inland Sea. This inlet from the Pacific is divided into two narrow straits by the little island of Avadji. I took the southernmost of the two, which is also the narrower and therefore where the current flows stronger – at an average of seven to eight knots, with a maximum of ten knots. I had to wait for three hours, until the current was flowing favourably for me, as there was no question of sailing against it.

But once into the Inland sea, all was calm sailing or rather drifting. I let the current carry me in the direction I wanted to go, then dropped anchor in a little bay of some pretty island before the current turned. The weather was splendid. It really is a most delightful region; the many hundreds of islands have great variety, and oddly enough neighbouring ones are sometimes the most different. Some islands are

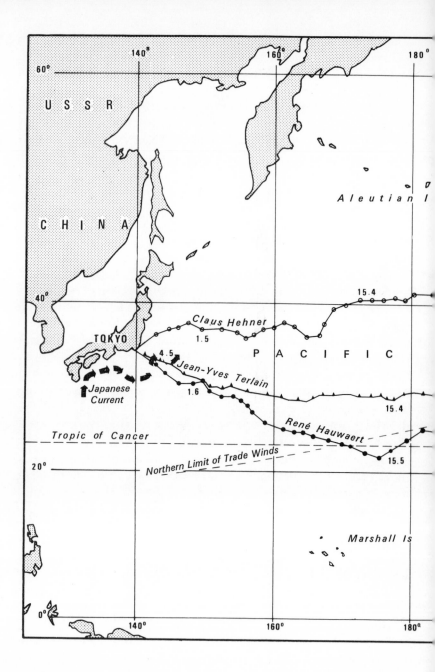

Routes of other
competitors in the
Transpacific Race

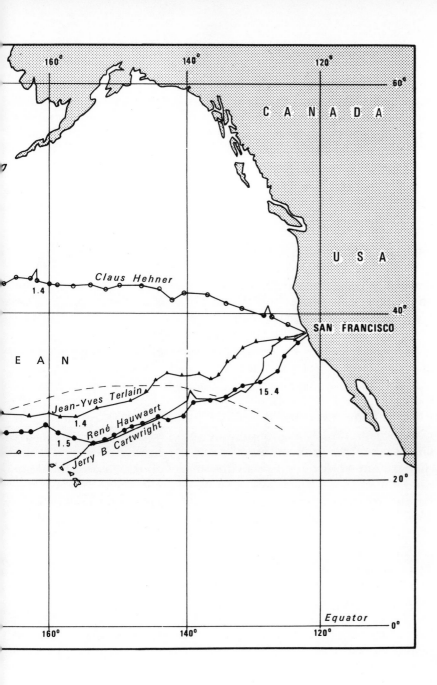

very green, others quite bare; some are low lying, others very hilly. I can't say that I saw the one which was the location of The Naked Island but I saw several that vividly reminded me of that film. It would all be a perfect paradise if the continual sound of engines did not spoil everything. The big ports and industrial centres round the Inland Sea mean that there is a constant flow of shipping, from huge tankers to small coasters, almost as constant as the traffic along a main road, without counting the swarms of fishing vessels working these waters and which seem to have the most clamorous engines in the world. Consequently, wherever you may be, it's impossible to get away from the rattle and din, night or day. In addition, much of the sea is dirty. Despite the lovely sunshine, on only three occasions did I find the waters tempting enough to have a swim.

I spent six days cruising about the Inland Sea. I had reckoned on being away from my base for about a fortnight. This was not long, but on the other hand there was Pen Duick IV and my crew waiting at San Francisco, the centreboard had still to be repaired, and the Los Angeles to Honolulu race was due to start in little more than a month.

The current carried me halfway along the Inland Sea and then it was time to turn back. Still in a flat calm, I reached the narrow strait I had come in by and, very early one morning, the current carried me speedily out into the Pacific again. I began to have a little wind at last. It was coming from the south-east and I had to keep tacking. It freshened steadily throughout the morning, so that I was shortening sail all the time. I took one and then a second reef in the mainsail and changed one jib for another. By the afternoon there was a fifty knot wind, the strongest I had ever experienced while sailing Pen Duick V. For the first time, I hoisted the No 3 jib. Under this small sail and two reefs in the mainsail, the boat maintained a good speed despite the rough sea. I had just about reached the area where I had taken a drubbing on the way out, after leaving Tanabe. And the wind was again dead on my nose. When evening came it was still blowing a strong gale and in addition the rain was pelting down in a manner that promised no good. I had previously experienced such weather only during very heavy thunderstorms and the cyclone I had run into off New Caledonia, and I had no wish to play around with a typhoon, if that was coming up. Next month was the typhoon season, but there had already been several. I could probably have made Tanabe, which must have been almost dead ahead and not far distant, but the wind direction would be making that harbour a dubious shelter. Instead I bore away to put into a bay that I had already passed, round a headland. Actually this bay was more like a fjord, long and narrow and with mountainous sides, and winding enough to be sheltered from all the winds that blow. I had the wind abeam and was planing fast as I made for its entrance. At about one in the morning I hove to at the head of the bay, which was full of coastal vessels that seemed to have run in here to wait for the storm to give over.

I woke at six next morning to find that the wind had hauled right round and was now favourable. I had breakfast and then got under way. Out in the open there was still a strong wind, but much less than the previous day. If it held, I should have a good run. The bay looked really lovely, bordered by jagged, contorted mountains typical of the country. All this coast is magnificent, very high and indented, and very windy.

The good following wind carried me about a third of the way to Tokyo that day, and at about midnight I moored in the bay of Goya. This bay, as I saw at daylight, is not very beautiful but is one of the biggest centres of the Japanese pearl-oyster industry. It is a very large bay and is given over entirely to oyster cultivation. But this was probably not the right season to see divers at work, for although I sailed about between the beds for some time there was no sign of activity. At the end of the morning I left the bay and continued up the coast to the bay of Tokyo and Aburatsubo.

I had a freshening southerly wind on the quarter and so made good speed. During the night the wind steadied at a good thirty knots, and all next day I was planing over the water. I had a race with a small coaster which, like others of her kind, must have been making about ten knots. Early in the afternoon I sighted her about three miles ahead of me, and at nightfall she was a mile astern. I think I must have roused the crew's interest when I was level with them, for I saw them on the bridge taking turns at looking at me through binoculars. I myself should have loved to see Pen Duick V planing along from a distance – it must be quite a sight. They hoisted a signal, but as I did not have the international code book I never knew what they were saying to me.

There was a glorious sunset that evening, and in the distance I could see the perfect cone of Fujiyama outlined against the deep red sky.

In the morning the wind had fallen and I made a very slow approach to Aburatsubo, taking good care not to get entangled again in the fishing nets set near the harbour entrance. Earlier during my stay I had been returning to harbour under spinnaker and with a good breeze, not thinking about these nets, and was almost upon them before I suddenly saw them, just as I was about to start taking in the spi. I put the helm right down, to take the wind out of the spi and check the boat's speed. The wind gradually drove me towards the nets, which were set permanently, with strong steel cables and iron floats. The keel, fortunately, caught on a cable between two floats. Fortunately too, the fresh breeze catching at the spi heeled the boat over enough for the keel to slide over the cable. The same thing happened with another cable, and then I was free of the wretched nets. There are very many of them all along the coast, and one can't be too much on one's guard against them. They are not marked on the charts, and at night very few have warning lights. To crown it all, Aburatsubo is the most important centre for pleasure craft in the country, and yet getting into or out of harbour at night is impracticable for anyone not knowing exactly where the fishing nets are set.

It was time to think about returning to San Francisco. I had hoped to find a buyer for Pen Duick V in Japan, for I did not need this boat any more. Selling her would relieve me of the worry of shipping her back home, and also – more important – enable repayment to be made to the St Raphael Yacht Club. Alas, Japan is not the best place for selling a boat, I found. Sailing as a sport is still in its early stages of development, and moreover there are heavy taxes (forty per cent) on boats exceeding a length overall of 24 feet 6 inches. That explains why they are all 24 feet 6 inches, most of them without any overhang fore or aft in order to have as much accommodation as possible. For these reasons, it was by no means easy to find a buyer for Pen Duick V.

However, there was one possibility. The Art Life Society, which had sponsored the race, had contacted a Japanese aluminium company that was thinking of buying the boat but first, naturally, wanted to look over her. I at once arranged to meet the company's representatives. Then I packed up the things I wanted to send back to France, and gave them to Jean-Yves Terlain, who had succeeded in selling his boat. Ten days went by and my meeting with the prospective buyers kept being postponed. I could not wait any longer; there was no time to spare if I were to have Pen Duick IV ready for the Honolulu race. And so I left Tokyo by plane without having met these people. Perhaps it was all a subtle Japanese joke! But Mr Ogimi, the secretary of NORC, promised to follow up the matter for me, and in any case to try to find a buyer for Pen Duick V. He is a charming man with a great knowledge of sailing craft, the sea and the problems of ocean racing. Competitors will always find him very welcoming and most helpful in solving any difficulties.

13

The Los Angeles
to Honolulu record

Back in San Francisco my crew must have been thinking I was having too good a time in Japan. As soon as I rejoined them we sailed Pen Duick IV seventy miles up river to the Colberg boatyard at Stocktown; this was the nearest boatyard working in light aluminium that we had been able to find. Fortunately the Renault agent in San Francisco very kindly lent me a motor car, which was a great help as we went out to the boatyard every day to see the work being done on the boat. When the centreboard was taken out, I realised why it had broken. This was a fairly easy matter to put right, and I took the opportunity to have the shape of its base modified, making it elliptical instead of straight. The area was thus increased, which ought to improve performance. But we were never able to draw it up completely; the elliptical base always protruded below the hull. However, this was no real disadvantage, since the rudder's draft (I was thinking of when sailing through shallows) was slightly more than that of the centreboard when drawn up.

After Pen Duick IV had been put afloat again I soon found that the centreboard was more effective than before. This was particularly noticeable after tacking. The boat did not go to leeward for so long and therefore regained speed more quickly. San Francisco Bay is splendid for a trimaran; there is usually a strong wind, but the waters are smooth – ideal conditions for sailing at a high speed. We went out several times with sailing friends we had made in the city, French and Swedish as well as American. We easily reached speeds of eighteen knots, touching nineteen and even twenty knots at times. Unlike planing over the swell out at sea, there were no waves in the bay and this high speed could be maintained provided the wind was fairly strong.

Our American friends were quite impressed, and they were experienced yachtsmen who know a boat when they see one. In San Francisco bets were being made on our attempt to beat the record and on whether we would make a faster time than Windward Passage, the

93   One of the crew
aboard Pen Duick IV

favourite for the monohull race. The odds were against us. American
yachtsmen were still prejudiced against multihulls; but those who went
sailing with us said they were going to put their money on us. I haven't
seen any of them again since the race but I hope they won plenty, for
Pen Duick IV reached Honolulu twenty hours ahead of Windward
Passage – which, as expected, won the monohull race.

There was only a very light breeze for the start of the race at Los
Angeles, but that was nothing unusual, for the winds are always very
light in those regions. In order not to hinder the monohulls we crossed
the starting line one hour after them, that is to say at 13.00 on July 4.
All afternoon, close hauled in a slight breeze, we kept overhauling
competitors. By nightfall we were up with the class A boats, but had
not yet sighted the largest of them, Windward Passage and Blackfin.
Soon after dark the wind freshened and veered, and we had it abeam;
so Pen Duick IV was making a comfortable thirteen knots. I thought
we should take the lead during the night, although by then we had seen
the lights of only one other competitor, whom we had overhauled. We
were approaching the area of the Trade Winds, and we set the big
spinnaker when the wind became more favourable. For the next

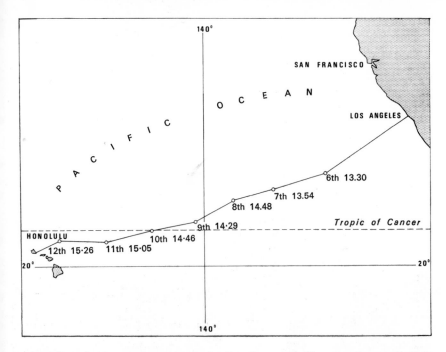

twenty-four hours we were under spinnaker and all was going well. But
then the spi had the wind spilled out of it as the boat was planing over
a wave – as happened now and again – got caught on a batten of the
mainsail and tore. We got it in and set the light spinnaker, but this had
little pulling power – partly because of the lightweight material, but
above all because it was old and worn. However, the wind was not very
strong and I thought it would hold while I was mending the heavy spi.
I had hardly finished that job than the light spi also tore. It was no
good at all now – to repair such a large tear in a sail as worn as that one
would be a sheer waste of time. We spread the heavy spi again; but
during the night it again got caught on a batten of the mainsail, and
this time the damage was too great for it to be mended with the
equipment available on board.

Our chances of beating the record for the crossing and finishing
ahead of Windward Passage suddenly seemed to have diminished. We
ought to have had more spinnakers with us for a race of this kind; but I
hadn't had the means to buy any more. The three we started with had
all been taken from Pen Duick III and were rather on the small side,
but we had to make the best of them. Now we were left with only the
very small spi, the heavy weather one, of 1,180 square feet (whereas the
spi that had just got badly torn had an area of 1,825 square feet). This
loss of sail area had an effect on speed, of course. We kept this small spi

94 Pen Duick IV's
progress

95 Pen Duick IV close
    hauled off Honolulu

spread all the way to Honolulu, but I reckoned that we took about twelve hours longer than we should otherwise have done, for the winds were generally not very strong. However, we achieved what we had set out to do – the previous record for the crossing was beaten by twenty-four hours and, as already mentioned, we finished twenty hours ahead of Windward Passage.

Despite this success, Pen Duick IV failed to find a buyer, though the owner of Windward Passage showed great interest in her; the day he arrived in Honolulu he told me he wanted to buy her. He was telling everyone that he would take the boat to the Bahamas, where he spent part of the year. But alas, he changed his mind when, I think, he saw the accommodation. He didn't say as much, but the reasons he did give for not buying her were not very convincing, and I feel sure that he was put off by the cramped accommodation. He was not, of course, expecting to find anything comparable with the comforts aboard Windward Passage – air conditioning, salt water extractor, etc, – but nevertheless the lack of space must have surprised him.

So I was left with two boats to get back to France. Pen Duick IV would be sailed back, and Pen Duick V would have to be shipped on a cargo vessel. I had hopes that the latter would not cost me too much. French shipping companies had in the past been very generous and helpful. The Compagnie Générale Transatlantique had given free transport to Pen Duick II and also Pen Duick V, as well as to Jean-Yves Terlain's Blue Arpège; and a German merchantship had taken Claus Hehner's Mex from Tokyo to Hamburg. The only expense was to have a cradle made for the boat, which was most necessary for her to be secure on deck. But now both the French shipping companies serving Tokyo, the Messageries Maritimes and the Chargeurs Réunis, definitely refused to help me. My luck was out, and the Transpacific race was going to be a costly event for me. If I sold Pen Duick V in France it could only be at a loss on the cost of building her. The race ought to have been in the opposite direction. In San Francisco I should certainly have had every chance of selling the boat at a good price, which would also have saved me a large sum to ship her home.

14
Reviewing the Transpacific race

I had reckoned on crossing the Pacific in forty days, and this I did to within a few hours, but it was a coincidence. I met with far less favourable winds than expected according to the predictions of the pilot charts, and consequently I ought to have taken longer. The difference was compensated for by the fact of the boat sailing a little faster than I had thought she would. In more normal wind conditions I would expect to sail the same boat across in at least three days fewer. Moreover, Pen Duick V had not been fully tested before the race, and another couple of days could probably be knocked off the time if the difficulties I had due to faulty equipment were eliminated.

These difficulties were due chiefly to three things – the self-steering gear, the telescopic booms and the ballooner headsails. As was obvious, the self-steering gear in itself functioned perfectly and was strong enough to stand up to the task, as it was still as good as new on reaching Tokyo. Nothing had broken, nothing had worn through or got rusty, and there was no play in it at any point. If this piece of equipment had been mounted differently, all would have been well. It needed placing on a framework extending about three feet farther aft; this would have prevented its rudder from being affected by the water disturbed by the boat's rudder, which was a cause of its imperfect performance, and the greater leverage would have improved its efficiency to the point of steering the boat in all conditions.

Several defects in the telescopic booms became evident during the crossing. In the first place, the pins holding the extensions in place were too sharp and several ballooners and spinnakers got torn on them. I had to spend a considerable amount of time in mending these sails, and of course I was deprived of their use during that time. Secondly, the slanting position of the booms, resting on the pulpit, made them difficult to handle when there was a swell on or the sea began to heap up; and their ends sometimes dipped into the water when they were fully extended. Moreover, it was impossible to regulate the length while keeping them braced – which would have been very useful. For instance, when the wind hardened I could reduce the balloner with the aid of its roller furler, but the length of the boom had to be reduced too. On the lee side the boom needs to be shortened as much as possible so that it does not dip into the water as the boat rolls and heels. But I could not reduce the length of the boom without first hauling down the balloner or rolling it up completely (if the gear had worked properly) and resting the boom on the pulpit. And all that took a lot of time. When the wind eased, just as much time was taken in extending the boom so that the balloner could be increased.

The ballooners had been made of sailcloth that was much too thin, and this proved a double disadvantage. In the first place, they were too fragile; but when I had them made I was not thinking of setting them in such fresh winds nor expecting such a strain to be put upon them. Secondly, I could not get them to roll up entirely because of the limited length of cable that the drum could take. If the sail had been of thicker material, fewer turns would have been needed to roll it up and the length of cable would have sufficed. Sometimes, in a strong wind, I could not get more than half the sail rolled up. The stronger the wind, the more tightly the sail rolled up – in other words, less of its area got rolled up for the same length of cable wound round the drum. Even breaking out the sail to lessen the strain was of little help; in fact the sail was then by no means easy to get in.

If I had been able to give the boat more prolonged trials before the race, these faults could certainly have been remedied in time. Then the handling of the boat during the crossing would have been simpler and less time would have been lost. That being said, I think Pen Duick V has proved to be a very successful boat, very fast on all points of sailing and especially, as expected, with following winds. But even when close hauled she sailed better than I had hoped.

Her one defect was the excessive slamming when sailing to windward in a big sea. It did not affect her speed but certainly made life uncomfortable on board.

The ballast tanks proved to be remarkably effective. There was no problem, though I must admit that pumping one pair of tanks full was good physical exercise. When the wind was very variable it even became a little wearisome. Sometimes I had to fill and empty them three or four times in twenty-four hours. Fortunately not every day was like that. There again, with more time available back in France, I might have found a pump with a faster flow.

The future of the boat is undecided at the time of writing. I might well be able to sell her in France at a fair price. The low headroom, which limits the accommodation possibilities, is obviously a factor against her. But to judge by the manner in which most people make use of their boats, this should not be too detrimental. About fifty per cent of boats are taken out only for the day and do not leave their home port, where the boat's owner often has a house. What then is the point of these boats being encumbered with spacious accommodation? In my opinion it is preferable to sail a very fast, lively boat and make do with bare necessities in the way of accommodation, just to be able to sleep aboard when occasion requires. Perhaps the ballast tanks can be a bit of a nuisance when on a cruise, but there is no necessity to retain them. It is simple enough to increase the weight of the ballast keel.

This is what I shall do if I don't succeed in selling the boat quite soon. For in that case I should use her for ocean racing, and as ballast tanks are not allowed I would have to fit a heavier ballast keel instead. There is no great problem about such a change, and it ought not to have too adverse an effect on the boat's performance. But everything depends upon the handicap rulings, which have recently been modified. If Pen Duick V's rating is suitable it might be entertaining to compete with her, although my preference is naturally for a bigger boat.

The bigger the boat, the more interesting ocean racing becomes and the sport benefits. When it is no longer a matter of the solo sailor, a number of factors are brought into play which call for high and complementary qualities to master them. In short, the team spirit is brought to the fore; and each member of the crew needs to have a complete knowledge of his allotted task. Any faulty handling of a small boat can easily be made good, but on a big boat it can have serious consequences straight away, because the power being deployed is so much greater than men's strength, and can even be dangerous. If a mistake does not cause something to break, time and energy will still be needed to put matters right. Mistakes in handling are only avoided if each member of the crew knows exactly what he has to do; one inexperienced man on a big boat can soon become a danger. Knowledge and experience apart, handling a big boat calls for more physical effort and therefore a stronger crew than on a small boat. A woman may be a very good crew on a small boat, for women are very attentive in general, but on a big boat the physical effort required would be beyond them most of the time. Regrettable though it may be, there's no getting away from the fact that the best and most attractive of ocean racing is necessarily confined to men. And what a splendid sight is a full crew racing a big boat with hardly a word being exchanged!

In any case, Pen Duick V has been a useful experience; and the big boat I am now thinking of building for handicap races – with a crew and also for solo sailing – will owe much to Pen Duick V. I shall ask the same architects, Michel Bigoin and Daniel Duvergie, to design her.

But what of the Transpacific race itself? The very nature of it makes this an attractive event. It is long, and the variable winds call for much handling and sail changing, especially over the final third of the distance. These conditions make it a good test of stamina; but nevertheless it is not such a hard race as the Transatlantic. Comparing the two, the shorter distance of the Transatlantic is more than offset by the prevalence of headwinds and the rough weather.

The organizers of the Transpacific are quite right, I think, not to open the race to both monohulls and multihulls. The object of an ocean race is a human contest, to compare the men sailing the boats, and such a comparison becomes quite arbitrary when boats so very different are being raced. That amounts in fact to having two different races over a course and distance which sometimes vary from one competitor to another. This is a criticism which can also be applied to the Transatlantic race. In that, the monohulls compete between themselves as they take the northern route, encountering difficulties that are well known, while the multihulls have obvious reasons for taking the southern route and escape those difficulties. A multihull increases speed by several knots when no longer obliged to sail close to the wind, whereas a monohull hardly increases speed at all. It is therefore to the advantage of a multihull to take a longer route if slightly more favourable winds might then be found which would result in a good increase in her speed. On the other hand, a monohull benefits from taking a more direct route. In a few years' time, when multihulls have given proof of their superiority – which they have not yet done – the Transatlantic will become a race for multihulls contested over the southern route, and this will take out of the race some of the toughness which has so far distinguished it.

I find myself less in agreement over the rule to limit boats for the Transpacific race to a length overall of thirty-five feet. By making us compete in such small boats the organizers eliminate some of the sporting interest of the race. What I have written about ocean racing by crewed boats is even more applicable to solo sailors. But if, as I maintain, the boat should be as long as possible, it is obvious that there must be a limit. I do not think one can yet say with any certainty what is the optimum, the most favourable size. There are some who believe in very big boats and even envisage an eighty foot boat with three masts. I have had no experience of such a rig, but that doesn't seem to me the ideal boat. The more masts there are, the less the results from a given sail area when close hauled. Such a boat might be valid for a race in which following winds predominate, but probably not for a race like the Transatlantic where one is sailing to windward most of the time. Personally my inclination is for a boat of about sixty-two feet maximum, schooner rigged.

At all events, on a boat of that size the strength and stamina of the man become of prime importance in obtaining the best possible results from the means at hand. His seamanship needs to be very good too, for he has to anticipate changes in weather conditions; he must not be caught napping by bad weather when there are large areas of canvas to handle, for getting them in would become too involved an operation. These are problems which do not occur aboard small boats. With them, what counts is the competitor's sea-going experience, his race experience, ability to do without sleep, and especially – if the race is a long one – that tenacity so necessary for maintaining the competitive spirit. You have to keep telling yourself, even in the worst moments, that every minute matters; for every change in conditions calls for a manoeuvre to keep the boat at her best speed. This necessity applies to all ocean races for solo sailors, but is more difficult to maintain on a big boat where fatigue increases in proportion to the greater energy expended and so the temptation to take a rest becomes more pressing.

There is therefore no more severe test than sailing a big boat singlehanded in an ocean race. In ocean races between crewed boats, each has a skipper to make decisions on tactics, sail changes and so on, a navigator to plot the boat's course and keep the skipper informed about currents and weather forecasts, etc, and a crew to take turns at the helm and to handle the sails. Each member may be a specialist in his particular role, yet not very good at standing in for someone else. A good skipper or navigator, for instance, might not necessarily be much good as crew – and the opposite applies. But the singlehanded sailor has to fill all these roles himself and endeavour to be very good at each of them. And when sailing a big boat he must in addition be perfectly fit physically. It is then one man against another, and the importance of the part played by the equipment is proportionally less than when sailing a small boat; in other words, the man's qualities and capabilities are predominant.

The organizers of the Transpacific race, in limiting the length overall to thirty-five feet, probably argued that by imposing this limit there would be more likelihood of attracting a good number of entries, for prospective competitors would have less difficulty in obtaining a boat if the cost was relatively low. I'm not at all sure that this argument can stand up to the facts. Nowadays, many solo sailors succeed in obtaining financial backing. Half the competitors in the last Transatlantic race (1968) had their boats paid for either by newspapers or by big commercial firms. And a good number of the large boats built for the Transatlantic race could have been used in the Pacific.

At all events, this San Francisco to Tokyo race is very interesting, and it attracted a good number of prospective competitors – fifteen were mentioned at one time. In the end, many of these withdrew, which was a great pity. It is to be hoped that next time there will be many more competitors to pass under the Golden Gate.

Appendix

The competitors and placings in the Transpacific race (based on a report in The Spray, the bulletin of the Slocum Society)

1   Eric Tabarly (Pen Duick V)
    Date of finishing: April 24, 20.59 hours
    Time taken: 39 days 15 hours 44 minutes
    Distance covered (approx): 5,700 miles
    Average speed: six knots

2   Jean-Yves Terlain (Blue Arpège)
    Date of finishing: May 5, 15.58 hours
    Time taken: 50 days 10 hours 43 minutes
    Distance covered (approx): 5,600 miles

Terlain knew that his boat was slower than either Tabarly's or Hehner's, so he put his hopes in the route along the northern limit of the Trade Winds, thus shortening the distance.

He picked up the Trades on latitude 28 and stayed on that parallel until he reached longitude 155 west, when he headed up for Tokyo. He made his landfall at the level of Nojima-Saki, but was then becalmed and the current carried him fifteen miles to the west. However, he reached the finish next day, aided by a 35 knot south-westerly wind.

Terlain's best week was the third, after picking up the Trade Winds. He covered 1,070 miles that week. His best run in twenty-four hours was 180 miles, when he was farther west but still on latitude 28, during his sixth week out, with good following winds. He ran into a gale during the first week, but had calm, clear weather for the rest of the crossing, except for one day shortly before the finish.

His self-steering gear was the same as Tabarly's, and he said he was perfectly satisfied with it, even with the wind astern. His sytem of twin headsails worked very well, but his sails proved too light for the weather conditions he had during the crossing.

3.   Claus Hehner (Mex)
     Date of finishing: May 7, 21.18 hours
     Time taken: 52 days 16 hours 3 minutes
     Distance covered (approx): 5,000 miles

Hehner chose the northern route, the Great Circle, hoping to beat Tabarly by reducing the length of his crossing.

He followed this route for the first week but then met headwinds of up to 58 knots and constant squalls, so he altered course to the west, sometimes heading south, and reached latitude 40 north of Hawaii. He stayed on that parallel for about eight hundred miles, and when north of Midway began to follow the Great Circle again. It was about then that he sighted his one and only ship during the whole crossing, a Philippine cargo vessel.

He crossed the international date line on April 11, two days before Tabarly. His best run in twenty-four hours was 164 miles, against headwinds. In fact he had the wind astern for only one day during the whole crossing. In the later part he met with gale force winds for eleven successive days; his self-steering gear was damaged and he had to manage without it for the rest of the time. The watertight collar at the foot of the mast came away and water streamed into the cabin, and to cap it all his radio direction finder was damaged and he was unable to take a bearing. This was very serious at the time, for he was in the path of the Black Stream and prevented by cloudy weather from taking a star sight. His storm jib got torn too, and for several hours he had to stay hove-to.

Despite all these difficulties, he made his landfall to the north of Tokyo and continued down the coast under spinnaker, with a light following wind, towards the finishing line.

An hour before crossing it, he was surprised by a forty knot southerly wind while negotiating the shipping entering and leaving the bay of Tokyo, and had a final tussle to get in his spinnaker while keeping an eye on the vessels all about him.

These first three were all veterans of the Transatlantic race. One of the other two competitors, Jerry Cartwright, was obliged to retire; and the fifth René Hauwaert, finished much later, a month behind Hehner.

Jerry Cartwright had the misfortune to be thrown out of his bunk during a squall, and banged his head on the edge of the other bunk. It was a hard blow on the ear, this brought on nausea and a complete loss of his sense of balance. He had to summon up all his courage and stamina to get to Pearl Harbour, where he was at once taken to hospital. For some days he suffered from dizziness and bouts of sickness and on medical advice he retired from the race. It was a great disappointment, for he had set his heart on the race, even though his boat did not seem in the same class as the others.

René Hauwaert was rather different from the other four. This young Belgian engineer who specialized in refrigerating plant had been working in the Congo when, like Louis van de Wiele, he heard the call of the sea. He bought an old, but sturdy ketch Vent de Suroît, and sailed away to Tahiti, where he spent many happy months. When ashore he still rides about on a woman's bicycle decorated with plastic roses, which was a present from a Tahitian woman. He never thought of winning the Transpacific race, only of reaching the finish. When only a few days out from Los Angeles he found that his mizzen rigging needed some repairs, but he calmly had lunch before starting on the job. His boat had been inspected by the organizers before the start of the race and passed as fit for the crossing.